A Vision of HOPE

addressing prejudice and stereotyping in the wake of 9/11

Reflections on Turning Ignorance into Understanding

International House, Berkeley is one of several organizations to respond successfully to a call from the Chevron Corporation for proposals to address the prejudice and stereotyping experienced by individuals and groups throughout the world in the wake of the September 11 attacks upon the United States. International House launched a major Narrative Essay Competition entitled "A Vision of Hope – Addressing Prejudice and Stereotpying in the Wake of 9/11," which has culminated in this collection of winning essays for national and international distribution.

International House wishes to express its great appreciation to the Chevron Corporation for inspiring and generously supporting the production and distribution of this publication.

"Funny in Farsi
by Dumas"

Cover illustration and book design by
Laurel Anderson-Malinovsky, 2005-6

Published by DF Publications, 1958 Vallejo St. #8, San Francisco, CA 94123, dflessons@aol.com.

Table of Contents

Introduction

"When you look at me, do you see me?"

These words from "Focus," a movie based on the short story of the same name by Arthur Miller, suggest for me an underlying theme of this collection of essays. The implication, of course, is that too often we are not really seeing clearly when we look at people. These essays are meant to help us "see" people beneath the physical surface and the often misleading associations that physical appearance suggests. In the wake of September 11, we saw how stereotyping based on physical appearance led to unjust victimization of many innocent people.

Hopefully, wide distribution of this publication, initiated and generously funded by the Chevron Corporation, will help to fill an ignorance gap and further mutual understanding and the intercultural educational principles of International House at the University of California, Berkeley.

Joe Lurie
Executive Director
International House, UC Berkeley

Salute to the 10 Bright Rays of Hope

Presumptuous. That was my reaction in taking up these essays for the first time. With a lump in my throat, I asked who am I to judge which essay was more deserving to be a winner when all these authors had courageously decided to bare their chests and humbly share with strangers their insightful and profound reactions to an event that had just turned the world upside down? As project director, I had myself struggled over the language I would use to describe and announce the essay contest. It was clear to me that to express the specificity and inclusiveness of what one really would like to convey, many words come only close to what one really means. The words *experienced, witnessed,* and *vicarious,* for example, all had to be used together so as to capture all the kinds of experiences we wanted to solicit from the contributors. Synonyms with all their different linguistic nuances could bring out issues of appropriateness, connotation, and perception. General terms such as *assumptions, bigotry, prejudice,* and *stereotyping* had to be carefully selected and utilized.

With this in mind, I especially applaud the authors of the essays selected for this collection for their vivid and revelatory language. They not only responded in a very personal fashion to the aftermath of 9/11 but incorporated in a non-didactic way concrete suggestions for changing attitudes and behaviors to counteract stereotyping, prejudice, and animosity. Thus, in their essays the authors are able to convey with poignant empathy and gut compassion what it means to be the "other." Their works offer us an insight into and an understanding of the subtle discriminatory practices resulting from others' reactions to one's looks, speech, and manners. They give us a sense of the inner drive of the individuals who have succeeded in overcoming these sometimes overt, most times subtle biases. Moreover, these essays effectively communicate the impact of invaded privacy, humiliation, and other personal affronts, which until experienced, are only peripherally understood.

How was all this done? Through an adroit interweaving of content and form, suspense, concrete visualization, among other techniques. The results are astonishing, clever, and heartwarming. No minimalism - the writers enter in and out of personal lives weaving in new criticality and aesthetics. Learn and unlearn as you read these remarkable ten visions of hope - challenging and uplifting retorts to some of the tragic effects of 9/11.

Liliane C. Koziol
Director of Programs, International House, UC Berkeley
Vision of Hope Project Director

A Few Words from the Editor

When my family and I first came to America in 1972, nobody had heard of Iran. Our move was temporary. My father had been given a two-year assignment to work with an engineering firm in Whittier, California that was building an oil refinery in Isfahan.

Growing up in Abadan, in Southern Iran, I had heard endless stories about "Amrika" and could not wait to see the country with my own eyes. My father had been a Fulbright Scholar in 1953 in Texas, so I had heard much about this magical place. My father always told us stories about big freeways, friendly people and very clean cafeterias. He had even told us that Americans put ice in their tea. That story, we never believed.

The Americans we encountered in 1972 were very friendly but knew almost nothing about the Middle East. People always asked us if we rode camels or lived in tents. They were surprised to hear that our life in Iran had many modern conveniences, including an air-conditioned Chevrolet. Despite the many questions about Persian cats and flying carpets, Americans welcomed us with genuine warmth. Ignorance about the Middle East did not hinder the hospitality and generosity.

All this changed on Nov. 4, 1979, when a group of Americans were taken hostage in Tehran, Iran. Overnight, bumper stickers and T-shirts declaring, "Iranians: Go Home!" and "We Play Cowboys and Iranians" appeared everywhere. The radio constantly played a song called "Bomb Iran." Overnight, the friendly America we knew disappeared and was instead replaced by an America we no longer recognized.

I was stunned by how quickly ordinary people turned to hatred. I realized that, sadly, many people learn about the world by watching the evening news. The problem is that only bad news is news. If we simply learn about one another from television, we see only images of war and famine. Humanity is never highlighted in the news, nor are the common, good, decent people who make up most of the world's inhabitants.

I knew then and there that I wanted to devote my life to highlighting our shared humanity, not just between Iranians and Americans, but amongst all people. I wanted to show that our commonalities far outweigh our differences. I became a writer.

When I was asked to edit a series of stories about the aftermath of September 11th, I immediately accepted. Like most people around the world, I watched the events of September 11th on television over and over again, unable to comprehend the horror. I knew that none of our lives would ever be the same, no matter where we are from.

The stories in this collection illustrate how ten individuals of the world, ranging from a doctor in Nigeria to a Sikh in California were affected by that fateful day and how they chose to react. None of the contributors are professional writers. They are ten individuals, each with a story, each with a vision of hope. They have chosen to share their stories in hopes that we can all somehow learn from one another. I hope you are touched by their words as much as I was.

Firoozeh Dumas
Editor, Vision of Hope Essay Contest
Author of *Funny in Farsi: Growing Up Iranian in America*

A Battered Renegade

Note: the author of this essay wishes to remain anonymous due to the unstable situation in the writer's country and for the protection of his/her life and that of family members.

I graduated from a medical school in Nigeria after eight years of undergraduate training and proceeded to do internship for one year. I was then posted for National Youth Service Corps, a one-year of volunteer service that all university graduates are meant to undergo. I was posted to serve in a predominantly Islamic state in northern Nigeria. After a three-week orientation camp, I was deployed to a comprehensive health center where I was to carry out my national assignment for the next year.

I returned to my homeland in the southern part of Nigeria four days after the end of orientation. As is customary for a child leaving his parents for a period of time, I received a lot of advice from my father and mother. My father, a lecturer in history and a devout Christian like the rest of the family, gave me learned commentary about the tradition and culture of the northern states of Nigeria. He said, "Sokoto state is the heart of the Islamic religion in Nigeria. There has been a long and bitter history between Christians and Muslims. Muslims still have memories of the massacres and desecration of their holy sites during the crusades and their subsequent expulsion from Spain and Portugal in the fifteenth century." He told me about Sharia, the Islamic law, and Jihad, the Islamic holy war. He told me about the Fulanis, Hausas and Kanuris, the three tribes that make up the population of states in the northern part of Nigeria. "These three tribes are predominantly Muslims, and they make up about seventy to eighty percent of the population of the northern states of Nigeria. They are hospitable people, fun to be with, especially when they have stayed with you for a period of time. However, they can behave erratically regarding religious matters," he said. It was quite an educative session.

The day of my departure finally arrived. Sokoto is about eighteen hours from my hometown. By 6:30am, I was ready. Mummy and Daddy drove me to the park, where I boarded a Toyota saloon car, a Japanese brand of car with four doors and a boot. I bade them farewell. Leaving my parents was not a pleasant experience. Right there at the motorpark, my mother could not hold her emotion and cried uncontrollably, knowing that I was going to a very strange land where religious riots have occurred before. My dad was sad on one hand that I was going to leave home for one year, but was happy that I was going to fulfill a compulsory national assignment.

We headed north on the Sokoto expressway. After about ten hours, it started to get dark. There were six men in the car, including the driver, all of us chatting as we went along.

The road to Sokoto unfolded layers of Islamic history, from early Muslim mosques to rounded thatched houses. Some huts were square and made of thick reeds instead of mud or grass. Women carried calabashes, large locally made wooden bowls on their heads. Nomads obstructed traffic with their herd of cows. Along the highway, women sold *fura da nono*, a Muslim drink made from fresh cow milk and wheat. It was a Friday evening and noise emanated from mosques. Muslims could be seen everywhere in their traditional attire. The men wore long flowing robes and long tunics that covered their bodies. The women wore Jilbab, an overcoat that covers from the neck to the feet, and Hijab to cover their heads.

We journeyed along, until it was nighttime. There were fewer cars on the road. We could now see innumerable stars in the sky and many trees along the road. Only the car engine was audible. As we drove, I thought about the many pilgrims who for uncounted generations had traveled on this same road.

Suddenly, the driver screamed and tried to apply the brake. There in the middle of the road stood a group of men, some with camels and others with horses. The car came to a stop. Two dark, stout men stood in front of us. They wore exquisite clothing, long flowing robes, and red shawls, and were corrugated with bandoliers, a belt worn over the shoulders for carrying bullets and knives. Crouched near them, four men pointed guns at us.

The group approached us, cheering wildly, galloping, curveting, firing shots and shouting. The crowd put on a wild and ragged show, whirling around our vehicle in a desperate chase, inducing clouds of dust so that our voices croaked. Eventually the parade ceased.

My neighbor, the passenger sitting to my right side, told me that the gang was part of a Muslim extremist group imbued with a deep antagonism towards non-Muslims and particularly hostile towards the west. They were nomads, though not pure enough to hold the nomadic code of honor or to obey the desert law in spirit and not villagers enough to have abjured the business of rapine and raid.

While we were still watching, all of us afraid, their leader asked his men to hold fire. The driver of our vehicle, with a merry laugh, sprang up and ran out towards them waving his full sleeve over his head in sign of friendliness. They shot him. He fell down and after a few minutes, gave up the ghost. Our fear heightened. I could now feel my heart beat in triple rhythm. My heartbeat pulsated up my throat, snaking into my sinuses and choking my breath.

The gang ordered us out of the vehicle and marshaled the remaining five of us in a straight line. Two riders trotting on camels came towards us from the north. They halted in front of us, and the more splendid one slipped gracefully to the ground without kneeling his camel. He threw his halter to his companion and ordered his men, "all of you, come and stand by me." They did as they were told. He strolled across and sat down, after glancing at the five of us with unaffected concern. He offered each of us a cigarette.

Lighting his cigarette, he said, "We are Muslims fighting for the justice of our brothers and sisters. Islam has suffered in the hands of other religions, particularly Christianity. Their brightest beacon, the United States of America, has massacred many Muslims, truncated so many lives midstream, and littered our communities with untimely graves. The September 11th 2001 attack on the United States made Americans even more heartless. America's reaction to the September 2001 attacks will forever remain green in our minds. We must retaliate," he said. "There are four other reasons for our anger and resentment against the United States: first, the American government's support for the Shah of Iran and complete opposition to the Iranian revolution, second, her unconditional support for Israel and the refusal to take significant steps towards the achievement of a Palestinian State. Third, the Gulf war, which was justified in the West by claiming to turn back Iraqi aggression but which was widely understood by Muslims as a means to prop up an autocratic, corrupt regime for maintaining American oil supplies. Fourth, threats to Islamic holy sites in Saudi Arabia and Jerusalem, resulting not only from American presence in the region, but from modernization and globalization, which threaten Muslim cultures. It is unfortunate that Christians around the world will pay for it." He ended his speech with a smile on his face.

I felt a shocking sensation all over my body, starting from my head, down to the soles of my feet. I suddenly felt feverish. Though a devout Christian, I needed to be a Muslim now to survive.

One of the gang members walked towards me and struck me on the head. He seemed curious about my intention and my history. My facial appearance looked like the Fulani's — I have a pointed nose, oblong face, elongated chin, fair complexion but no tribal marks. He asked me my religion. I said "Muslim." He started questioning me about Islamic principles and customs, the pillars of Islam, major beliefs and tenets. He asked me about the major Islamic festivals, Id-El Fitri, Id El Maulud, and Id El Kabir. He inquired about my family. I told him my mother is a Christian and my father a Muslim. Looking quite dissatisfied, he punched me in the stomach, then slapped me. He hit me on the leg so hard that I fell, my ankle trapped and twisted painfully.

I winced in pain. He then gave me a sharp kick over my left ear. I screamed. Though still conscious, I was in severe pain. I promised myself that if I came out of this alive, I would seriously increase my practical faith in God and try to find a lasting solution to situations like this. The decision did little to lessen the agony in my chest, but it gave me something to wake up for tomorrow. I rolled on the ground. I continued to scream. My attacker covered my mouth with his hand, stifling my scream. I breathed deeply through my nose and pulled my head backwards just a little. He then kicked me in my groin. I stopped screaming. Perhaps he thought I was unconscious. He then left me.

While lying still, in severe pain, I heard a gunshot. About two minutes later, another shot. Not too long after this, I heard a loud scream. I opened one of my eyes. It was the passenger that sat to my right side in the car. He was stabbed in the abdomen. Minutes later, he fell to the ground. His corpse rested against a tree, bleeding from the open wound.

Perhaps my colleagues stood their ground as Christians or claimed to be Muslims but could not prove it.

The attackers placed all the five corpses into our vehicle and drove off, heading northwards, laughing and chatting. I believe the little I knew about Islam, for which I credit my Muslim friends and my father, as well as my distance in the bush, and most importantly, God's divine grace and providence made me survive the incident. Perhaps I survived to tell the story.

I managed to sit up, my left ankle twisted at an odd angle. I grasped my leg and jerked it from beneath a piece of wood. What felt like fire rushed up my legs and into my brain, singeing my nerve endings. "Stand up," I ordered myself. Surprisingly, my body obeyed. My injured foot dragged behind me as I hopped along as quickly as I could towards the road.

I was later picked up by people I did not know after about six hours and taken to a nearby clinic. I was subsequently transferred to a hospital, where I stayed for two weeks. I had narrowly escaped death. I had survived one of the stranger episodes of my life, and learned some important lessons about religious prejudice and bigotry in the world. Perhaps I would have been killed like the others had I not claimed to be a Muslim. Only God knows how many innocent people have died throughout history for similar reasons.

I have thought of this experience, which occurred three years after the September 11th attacks, over and over again. The more I think of it, the more it shocks me. I have few illusions about the ruthlessness of the "enemy," whoever he is and however he is defined. I have tremendous admiration for those who risk their lives every day in situations worse than the one I faced. Never have I felt less secure.

The experience taught me some lessons, which will ever remain green in my mind. I saw the September 11th attack on the United States as having a religious background. The gang leader's conversation revealed this to me. I learned that religious intolerance is dangerous and we cannot afford it.

I learned that freedom of religion, freedom of speech, and freedom from fear, the so called essential human freedoms as embodied in the United Nations Declaration of Human Rights (UNDHR) adopted in 1948, are far from being achieved in most under-developed countries, especially in Africa. Human rights are not universal.

I learned that humans possess both good and bad ideals, and that a terrible fight goes inside everyone – a fight between two wolves. One is evil and represents hate, anger, arrogance, criticism and intoler-ance. The other is good and represents peace making, love, tolerance, understanding, humility, empathy and compassion. Which wolf wins is the one you feed.

My near death experience did not change my relationship with my Muslim friends. It only showed me that the personality of an individual matters. Each individual decides what he wants. I still have friends who are pious, but not to fanaticism.

The October 2004 incident affected my life in a number of ways. It made me increase my quest for knowledge, be it in the sciences, arts, religion or politics. I now see that no knowledge gained is wasted. My little knowledge of some Islamic concepts, pillars, laws, and the Quran, saved me from death. I now crave for knowledge in all aspects of life and will continue to do so.

Most importantly, the experience changed my view of my creator. God can save, if we can trust Him wholeheartedly. My trust in God increased after that incident. I have learnt to believe all God's promises and never to doubt His promises concerning me. God saved my life, and I will ever remain grateful to Him.

It is time for us to look back and condemn the religious intolerance seen in the world today. It is a time to look forward and dedicate ourselves as individuals to the creation of a just world, free of religious hatred and to uphold our faith to a high standard of love and justice. Our perception of God's light can guide or blind us.

We can insist on these in many individual and collective ways. We should all read a religious text from a faith not our own, and learn about other religions and cultures. We should negotiate to solve religious and political crises. Compromise does not represent abandonment of one's conviction, but rather evidence of our shared belief in civilized resolutions of our differences. These are great possibilities. They are highly desirable, and the major constraints to their realization are bound to diminish in the very near future. To achieve this, all Muslims, religious leaders, Christians, Jews, indeed every living being has a role to play. The human mind remains our fundamental resource.

And The Walls Came Tumbling Down

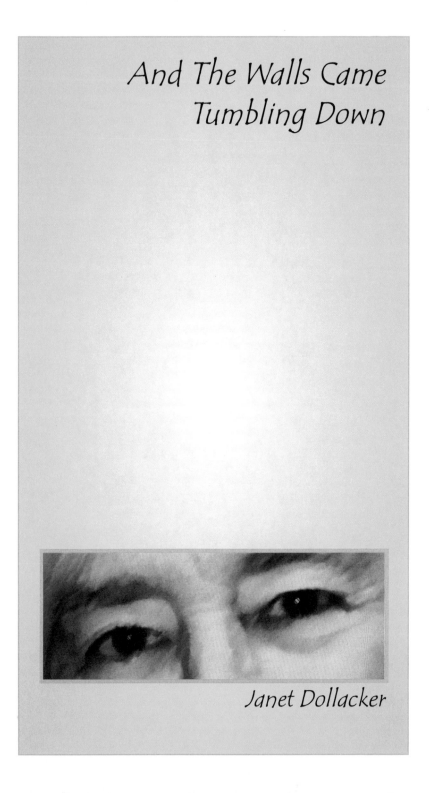

Janet Dollacker

We live in a country diverse not only in its race and national origins but in its political, philosophical and religious beliefs as well as its economic class and socio-cultural values. This diversity is at the same time our greatest challenge and our greatest strength. Like the opposing poles of electricity which are what cause it to work, or the polarity of male and female which enables us to survive, the scale of any act we do will range in value from death-dealing to life-giving energy. It is this yin and yang of life that offers us choice. A nation of much diversity is endowed with many choices and has just that much more potential for both good and evil.

On the day the twin towers exploded and imploded, all of our shadows, our differences, suddenly had the potential to be exposed to the sun. Some people were blinded by its glare and refused to see or acknowledge anything but their own overwrought feelings. Others reacted with guilt too quickly assigned (as almost happened with our own homegrown Oklahoma bombing), causing many of us to fear that this human tragedy would be politicized and/or form fitted into that old right-wing agenda called "the New American Century." We wondered what ever had happened to the previously much-publicized ticking of the nuclear clock.

It seems that most people, as long as their own lives are relatively safe and sound and they have enough to eat, tend to go along with whatever the powers-that-be decide. This is particularly true in America, where in the past the balance of powers between the legislative, the executive and the judicial has pretty much kept too much power out of too few hands. Yet, sitting here as I write, I am reminded of the enflamed rhetoric of William Lloyd Garrison, "The apathy of the people in a Democracy is enough to make every statue leap from its pedestal and hasten the resurrection of the dead!" And it surely must be true, that there is no tyranny that is as dangerous to the public welfare as apathy.

Fortunately my musings turned to Einstein who offers that message of hope in which I so much believe: "In the middle of every difficulty, lies opportunity." With time, more Americans are beginning to look at issues that they would never have even considered before 9/11. More Americans are beginning to take their responsibility as citizens seriously. And more of us are beginning to think in terms of the Brotherhood and the Sisterhood of mankind rather than in purely nationalistic terms. Small community groups are gathering all over our nation to discuss the political economic and global issues that affect us all and we are beginning to work together to put the kind of groundswell pressure on our government that only the massive voice of a diverse citizenry can bring to bear. We are asking one another serious questions about war and peace, about our primary values and how to implement them, about religious tolerance, about social justice.

It's not just talk. Groundswell groups are organizing all over the country to act on these American ideals. Just a few of the most effective secular groups come to mind: MoveOn.Org, United for Peace and Justice, Americans for the American Way, Democracy Now, The Nuclear Age Peace Foundation, and thousands of Yahoo groups, student groups, environmental groups and civil liberty organizations. Some of these such as the American Civil Liberties Union (ACLU) and Amnesty International have existed for years. Now that the importance of diversity of values and its long term effects on our diplomacy, economy, and environment is being perceived, great numbers of ordinary people such as schoolteachers, nurses, firemen, librarians, grandmothers and teenagers are getting involved with the great political discussions of our time and taking action. For peace, justice and equality to come about, this is the first and most important step.

One of the most important ways each of us can be more accountable to our world is to seriously consider what kind of world we would like to inhabit. Then we must consider what we can do to reach that goal, one small step at a time. As the Chinese say, "Even a journey of 1000 miles begins with the next step."

It seems to be an ill-fated human failing to remember the one complaint you receive among one hundred accolades. Following 9/11, it was two or three ugly incidents that stick in my mind and heart, notwithstanding the heroism of firefighters and private citizens as well as the beneficent concern of Europeans towards Americans stranded abroad without news from home. And maybe that is just another reason why we should each be cognizant of how lasting the effects of our words and acts can be.

Immediately after 9/11, I became concerned about the prevalence of a jingoistic rah-rah-rah brand of "cheerleader" patriotism, where

Image is more important than Reality. To me, that kind of patriotism brought to mind the now famous quip of Samuel Johnson," Patriotism is the last refuge of scoundrels."

Subsequent events would bear this out. This was the time when an Indian Sikh fled San Francisco for Arizona, thinking he would be safer outside of a major metropolitan area. (I could have told him that he was an Innocent if he thought the rest of the country more tolerant or safer than the San Francisco Bay Area.) Gathering up his things he left for a desert town in Arizona. He had only been there a week when an ignorant redneck "patriot" saw him walking along the street, mistook this turbaned Sikh for an Arab terrorist, ran home for his hunting rifle and shot him dead.

So many people were putting American flags on their cars that I began to stare into car windows to see what kind of people were driving these cars with the flamboyant flags. I was astonished to find that 8 out of 10 were foreign looking, Asians, Indians, Hispanics, or Middle Easterners. I realized they were scared, scared of being singled out and suspected of who knows what. My long time Indian and Islamic neighbors, small business owners and friends either sold their businesses and fled or fearfully and ostentatiously hung American flags everywhere they could. There used to be a Sikh owned grocery store a few blocks from my home, the only grocery store for miles. I went there the other day to buy some bananas and mangos and to chat for a while, only to find that they had sold it to second generation Mexicans. A few blocks down the road was the cheapest gasoline to be found in this gas guzzling society. It was owned by an Indian family. The last time I pulled up at the pump, I was told they were gone, out of the country, probably forever. And Nazrat, dear Nazrat, a very talented friend I had known for many years from the Marin Watercolor Society, had lived in America for over twenty years. When she heard about that East Indian man, a very popular high school teacher, gunned down in broad daylight in the high school parking lot, she packed up and moved to Switzerland. The slain teacher had been a much loved and highly respected member of the beautiful onion-towered temple that presides in splendor right above my home.

So this was the time when the shadow side of America became visible. There was a good side to this, however, because people began to raise questions and provoke discussions. There was a lot of talk in chat rooms and copy shops about the difference between nationalism and patriotism. New issues began to be examined such as:

1) What is the difference between Nationalism and Patriotism?

2) Is patriotism that old Nazi ego-trip whose slogan was "my country, right or wrong?"

3) Does patriotism mean I care enough about my country, its people, its values of diversity and democracy to be involved?

I began to realize that what had permitted an ignoramus to mistake an Indian for an Iraqi terrorist (at the time our government was desperately trying to link Iraq with the bombing of the World Trade Center) is the same viewpoint that permits this current regime to get away with its mischaracterizations. It is the same reason why so many of our citizens believe it is unpatriotic to disagree with the government. And this despite the fact that it was our own Thomas Jefferson who said, "The highest form of Patriotism is dissent."

There are actually two main causes. The first being the unlikely but common practice of identifying one's own self and one's country with whatever regime happens to be in power. The Bush regime is not America. America consists of her people, her history, her values, her energy and creativity, her struggles, her arts and music, her land from sea to shining sea and more. But if I were to believe that whatever current regime temporarily is in power, is America, then, it would be very difficult to see her faults. The faulty logic goes like this, "I'm a good person. I'm an American. The government is American; therefore it would not do anything that I myself would not do. And if it does, it must have some perfectly good and necessary reason that it just isn't able to tell me right now." I think this is also why good Germans, used to the cultured and civilized land of Bach, failed to foresee or even to be able to imagine the brutal tyranny of Nazism."

The other cause is our provincialism. Unlike Europe and the countries of the Middle East, America is geographically isolated from other perspectives. In France, I can drive two hours in any direction and be in another culture with a different outlook on life. Whereas in our own land, the further you get away from the coasts the more insular and homogeneous the culture becomes.

When you only know one way of life, then that becomes the standard. With the exception of the wealthy, many Americans who live in out-of-the-way places lead lives similar to the non-travelers of the middle ages, who also made a virtue out of their insularity, their conformity and their similarity to one another. Without diversity, there is no basis for comparison. There is a tendency to think that ours is the only right way and if other people aren't like us, they should be! Like Evangelical Christians, some see it as their prerogative, indeed their job, to spread the Good News that there is a Right Way and we know what it is. If they had come to Berkeley or to San Francisco they would have heard that the way is created by walking it.

I had a very dear friend who told me that the problem in America today is there is no longer any consensus, any unifying sense of values like we used to have in small towns. And I guess in a sense this whole essay is a response to that. If everyone thinks alike, no one is thinking. If we are all alike we become robotic and live on automatic drive. Water without input becomes stagnant and begins to stink. And no one and no one country can "have" the truth. The truth is a process, not a thing; a dynamic, multi-layered, interconnected, multicultured, diverse evolutionary discovery.

My other sad story has a happier ending. One beautiful fall day, the neighborhood spokesperson cornered me in my backyard and in hushed tones dripping with suspicion and fear asked me what I knew about my new next-door neighbor, Mohammed. "He keeps his blinds closed," she told me through pursed lips. "He hasn't moved his car in days. I never see him walking around or talking to anyone, ever, even once..." I put my finger to my lips and stopped her right there: "I thank God every single day," I said, "for this wonderful and perfect neighbor. He is clean and he is quiet. He never bothers anyone. And," I said pointedly, "he minds his own business." I continued before she could interrupt. "When Trudy, my previous next-door neighbor died, I was so worried about who would move into these relatively affordable condos that I couldn't sleep. We could have gotten heavy metal fans whose drums would have reverberated throughout the complex. We could have had drunken family rages. We could have had parties at three A.M. every weekend. We could have had drug dealers. And you worry that someone is reclusive and quiet, because his name is Mohammed? I wish we could have fifty more Mohammeds here!" She must have re-thought and re-broadcast her thoughts to the others, because I never heard another word about it.

Still slightly fuming a few hours later, I knocked on Mohammad's door and welcomed him to the complex with a loaf of homemade bread and a bit of salt, explaining that this is a lovely old Scandinavian custom to welcome a new neighbor. Even though I am not Scandinavian, I wanted to let him know he is among friends. The salt is to spice up life for good luck, I told him.

One year later I look around my complex and I see four more Muslim families, good neighbors all. We're lucky to have them.

The flower children from the sixties used to say that war is not good for people or other living things. Americans have not had a war on our own shores in any living person's memory. We are naïve. War is not about guts and glory and flags waving in the air. It's about a father scrambling for dear life, with his child clutched tightly to his chest, gasping for breath after miles of running and stumbling, only to look down in horror to see his son's neck limp, skin cold. It's about night terrors twenty years later, scars on the soul, buzzes in your head that never heal. People who know war do not glorify it. They do not do photo-ops in a borrowed parachute suit. The Republican five-star general from World War II, President Dwight D. Eisenhower said, "When people speak to you about a preventive war, you tell them to go and fight it. After my experience, I have come to hate war. War settles nothing."

Conventional wisdom seems to have it right that the fact of war is already proof of failure, that no one actually wins a war except perhaps for the re-constructors. One of the main problems with spending billions of dollars on war is that there is then nothing left for the peace and justice that helps to prevent wars. With all of the money spent on wars against "terrorism," if we truly are bent on making a world safe for democracy, we could put our heads together to design cultures that are people-friendly.

With the nuclear bomb looming over all of us, peace is the one condition of survival. As more and more people begin to see that there is no one right way, that there is no perfect country any more that there is any such thing as a perfect person, but that each has something to give that others lack, perhaps we will begin to listen to one another, to learn from our differences, to benefit from one another's strengths and to recognize that our differences are delightful! They are precisely what we have to offer one another.

We each of us, as individuals and as nations, have a truth, a vision to share. We are part of an enormous and beautiful quilt. All of us together can be engaged in forging a new paradigm for a better world where the real bottom line is no longer Winning is Everything and Winner takes All, but like all good families everywhere the real bottom line, the real foundation of a good society is "One for All and All for One."

Cultivating Compassion: a Response to Prejudice in the Wake of 9/11

Karen Erlichman

When I woke up at 6:03 AM on the morning of September 11, 2001, I felt as if I'd awakened from a nightmare. My heart was racing and my pajamas were damp with sweat. But I hadn't awakened from a nightmare; I'd awakened to one.

"I have a funny feeling," I said to my partner. "I don't feel right. Something bad must have happened."

We turned on the morning news, a daily ritual, and saw the footage of the World Trade Center after the first plane hit it. I sat at the foot of the bed stunned, mouth wide open. My brother and his wife were living only a few blocks away from the World Trade Center, soon to be known as Ground Zero. Without taking my eyes off the television, I reached for the phone and watched the second plane hit.

I tried many times to reach my brother by cell phone, house phone, pager, but couldn't get through. I called my mother in Philadelphia. She was crying and her voice sounded like a tiny squeaking toy.

"They're fine. They're safe. They're okay," she reassured me. And I exhaled.

"Where will you be today?" I asked. "I need to know where you'll be," I added.

For the next few weeks I had a desperate need to know the exact whereabouts of my loved ones. I needed to visually locate them in a specific place in order to feel anchored and at ease, especially with my family living three thousand miles away on the East Coast.

My partner had a medical appointment that day, so we drove into the city together. My clients had cancelled their appointments for the day, and it seemed that nearly everyone was parked in front of the television, computer or radio following the day's events.

As we sat in the doctor's waiting room, there was a woman on her cell phone talking at such a high volume that her voice was intrusive and grating. I kept waiting for her to end the call, but it seemed endless. The rest of the people in the waiting room kept looking at each other with frustration. Finally I got up, went over to the seat next to her, and in the softest, gentlest, most respectful way I could manage, requested that she take her cell phone out into the hallway. She looked at me indignantly and shook the cell phone at me, shouting, "Excuse me, but I have family in

New York. You don't understand."

"Actually I do understand," I replied. "I have family in New York too. But your loud voice is upsetting to the rest of the people in the waiting room." Outraged, she turned away from me, barked something into the phone about having been "rudely interrupted" by someone in the room, and ended the call as the receptionist called her name.

That acute tension, fear and reactivity was everywhere. If I heard a loud startling noise, I jumped and my heart fluttered. People seemed to be holding their breath.

I went to an interfaith prayer service that night, hoping to find some comfort and community. People from diverse races, religions, ages and families gathered in the tiny Half Moon Bay church to pray for peace and for those who had been killed.

The following day when I returned to work, it was overwhelming to sit with my psychotherapy clients and support them through their feelings and fears about the events of 9/11. At times I listened and witnessed their grief and anxiety, my own similar feelings were stirred up, and somehow I had to set them aside in order to be fully present and of service.

On September 13 I attended a class at the Mercy Center in Burlingame. It was the first day of a three-year spiritual direction-training program. As would be the case in every class, our day began and ended with prayer. Together we prayed for peace, led by the loving attentive presence of Sister Lorita and Sister Maryann. During a time of shock, sadness and despair, it was comforting to be part of a group of people from varied religious backgrounds coming together on our formation journeys as spiritual directors.

As a Jew and as a progressive political activist, I had a broad range of feelings and responses during the subsequent weeks. Given the long pernicious history of anti-Semitism, I had never deluded myself into thinking that anyone could be immune to targeted violence or hatred. At moments I even felt cynical about that. I had concerns about the reactionary patriotism that seemed to be encouraging xenophobia, racial profiling, mistrust of foreigners, and unbridled anti-Arab racism. An African American Muslim colleague stopped wearing the traditional Muslim head covering due to repeated harassment by airport employees, and other travelers. The sudden preponderance of American flags was a reminder of that nationalistic response, and was often accompanied by rhetoric that blatantly condoned racism, bigotry and stereotyping. I saw many bumper stickers with American flags and slogans that said, "America: Love it or Leave it," or "These Colors Don't Run," messages that were more judgmental and hostile, rather than peaceful and humane.

There was also a surge in the number of Americans attending services at churches, synagogues and other spiritual communities, and even New Yorkers were being nice to each other. There seemed to be a momentary sense of a collective us.

Several months later I started a new job as the Interfaith Outreach Program Director at Jewish Family and Children's Services in San Francisco. Since September 11, the agency had received an overwhelming increase in calls from people requesting crisis counseling. Some were Holocaust survivors and their family members, and others were from Jewish agencies and organizations requesting on-site support. The agency had arranged for someone to come to our staff meeting to provide "critical incident debriefing" for us, the clinical staff who were dealing with this deluge of need. Although we were the social workers responsible for supporting and caring for others, we had our own feelings and reactions as well.

We were also a building full of Jewish professionals and clients, including some Israelis, and Jewish immigrants who'd experienced the horrors of anti-Semitism in Russia and Eastern Europe. Fear and survival instincts were activated in nearly everyone. Building security was expanded, and we were all painfully aware of the huge sign in the front of the building with the title of the agency, Jewish Family and Children's Services. Although the anti-Arab racism far exceeded the current prevalence and intensity of anti-Semitism, nonetheless history had taught us that during times like this, anti-Semitism increases in frequency and severity.

Jews are often targeted and blamed for other acts of violence and political programs and the events of 9/11 were no exception. U.S. support for Israel was named as one of the causes of anti-American sentiment abroad. The growing anti-war movement that began coalescing in response to the invasion of Iraq was beginning to include nasty anti-Israel and anti-Jewish rhetoric. Some people have difficulty recognizing that the actions of the Israeli government do not represent the beliefs of all Jews or all Israelis. Poster boards were seen at some demonstrations that said things like "Hitler should have finished the job."

The events of September 11 and the U.S. invasion of Iraq presented a new, unexpected challenge for me. I've been a political activist for over twenty years, but most of my previous strategies for speaking out against injustice seemed insufficient in response to the increasingly conservative and bigoted political climate in the United States. The threat to our civil liberties was no longer a theoretical possibility; it was real. Although I continued to participate in street protests and letter writing, most of the time I felt inadequate and dissatisfied.

One overcast Saturday morning I attended an anti-war demonstration in downtown San Francisco. The streets and sidewalks were teeming with people from varied ages, racial and ethnic groups, and from all over California and the Western U.S. I had consciously chosen to wear my kipah, also known as a yarmulke, or skull cap, to the rally. I wanted to be visible as a Jew and as a person of faith, even though it felt risky and precisely because it was risky. Generally I wear my kipah when I am praying, when I am in a house of worship or attending a lifecycle event like a wedding or a funeral. I also decided to wear it to the rally because I wanted to integrate more fully the two different parts of myself, the spiritual and the political.

As I walked with the crowd toward the main stage of speakers, the sound of drumbeats, chanting and traffic hummed in my ears. To my surprise, I literally walked right into one of the nuns from my spiritual direction training program. Initially we were both startled, and hugged each other with joy and affirmation of our shared convictions.

On the other side of the street was a small counter demonstration with people carrying signs like, "If you don't like it here in America, then leave!" Some had poster boards with Biblical quotes and pro-military slogans. The feeling of camaraderie and optimism had vanished, and in its place I could feel the judgment and venom rising in me like bile.

I went to my monthly spiritual direction session and talked about how difficult it felt for me to pray for those people who were endorsing or engaging in acts of prejudice, bigotry and violence. My spiritual director shared with me a teaching from Thich Nhat Hhan, Vietnamese teacher, writer, peace activist and Buddhist monk, called "Compassion Meditation for the Person You Despise Most." I actually laughed with nervous disbelief as she shared with me the first time she used this meditation practice regarding a co-worker who had been treating her and others unkindly. She practiced this meditation daily for several months until she finally experienced a lightening of her spirit, a release of the judgment and resentment she'd felt toward her coworker. This did not mean she agreed with the person's beliefs or condoned his behavior. It simply meant that she experienced a relief from the burden of feeling judgment or hatred of another person.

I confess that I have not practiced that compassion meditation. Perhaps my practice is simply to remember that such a meditation exists. I strive to live my life with compassion at the center of everything I do, in my work, my relationships, my family and my community. As one of my teachers reminded me recently, the spiritual practice of engaging in struggle offers the possibility that the wound will eventually become the womb, the place of regeneration and renewal. Rachamim, the Hebrew word for compassion, comes from the same root as the word for womb, racham. Compassion is one of the fundamental teachings in nearly every faith tradition, transcending differences in theologies, beliefs and philosophies. Most major world religions teach some version of the Golden Rule, or the Ethic of Reciprocity. In Judaism, the Torah says v'ahavta l'reyacha kamocha, "love your neighbor as yourself." In Christianity, the New Testament says, "Therefore all things whatsoever ye would that men should do to you, do ye even so to them: for this is the law and the prophets" (Matthew 7:12.). In Islam it is said, "None of you [truly] believes until he wishes for his brother what he wishes for himself." (Number 13 of Imam "Al-Nawawi's Forty Hadiths)."In Native American Spirituality, Black Elk teaches that "All things are our relatives; what we do to everything, we do to ourselves. All is really One." And in Buddhism it is said, "Hurt not others in ways that you yourself would find hurtful" (Udana-Varga 5:18).

When I remind myself of this common thread of compassion that is woven through nearly every culture and faith tradition, I feel a sense of hope and optimism, especially when I see little evidence of this philosophy in the everyday reality of human behavior. I wish I could say that the political climate has improved, or that people in general have become more accepting and compassionate and less judgmental and prejudiced. Unfortunately, the media seems to focus primarily on continued acts of violence and hatred, ignoring or downplaying news stories about acts of compassion and kindness. Despite the initial post-9/11 surge in participation in religious services and interpersonal courtesy and kindness, many people seem to have reverted back to their old patterns of complacency, bitterness and isolation. Awareness of our mortality and human vulnerability seemed initially to engender more considerate and generous human interactions, in the grocery store or while driving. Sadly, this no longer seems to be the case. In fact, many people seem to be more guarded and more mistrustful than ever.

How do I maintain a sense of hope and compassion during such times of despair? I continue to listen to and support my clients who are dealing with similar feelings. I have begun talking with colleagues about how even psychotherapy and spiritual direction can be tools of social change as well as personal growth and healing. And I carry the description of Thich Nhat Hhan's compassion meditation in my journal every day.

New Vision

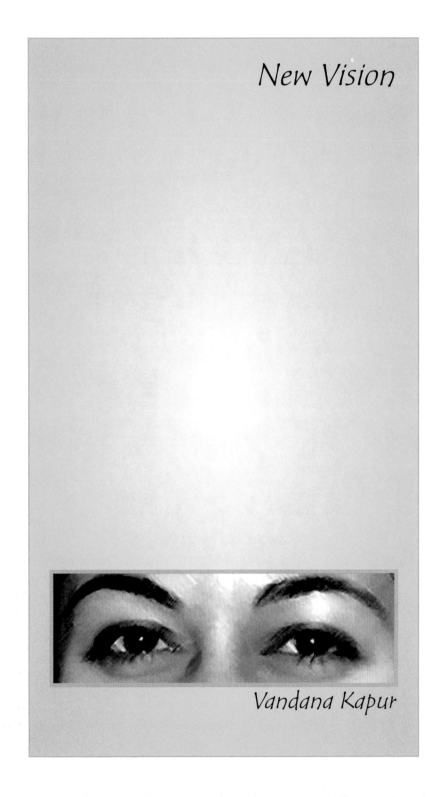

Vandana Kapur

The summer of 2002, following my senior year of high school, was one of the happiest and saddest times of my life. I was thrilled at the idea of finally moving on to my college career, a stage in my educational and personal life that I had been anticipating for as long as I could remember. As excited as I was about entering college, reaching that monumental point meant surviving my family's big move across the country. For career reasons, my parents were relocating from my lifelong home of Montgomery County, Maryland, to the unknown world of Arizona at same time that I was leaving for UC Berkeley. Most people could not understand why it made any difference to me — after all, I was moving across the country to California anyway. Yet for the few breaks that I would go back to visit family, my visits would be to a house, not a home. No longer would I see the familiar faces of friends and relatives. Street names and local restaurant names would be unfamiliar. It would be impossible to find any parks or playgrounds that reminded me of childhood, a time when all was good and right with the world.

The whirlwind of activities and emotions that preceded my family's departure still remains very much etched in my memory. Movers emptied the house. My family and I, originally from India, said our final good-byes to our only relatives in this country. My parents had been there for 21 years, the bulk of the time that they had lived in this country. At the airport, my heart ached from having to leave all of those wonderful people and the place that had nurtured me through childhood. I know that my entire family felt the same way as we sat silently at our designated gate, each of us depressed. We barely so much as stirred until we heard a call for passengers to board the plane.

When my family got up to walk through the security checkpoint, we were each asked to step aside. Back then were the days of "random" security checks, whereby those who were chosen for the searches tended to interestingly enough fit the profile of the typical Middle Easterner. Because I had already been subjected to these security procedures in recent flights, I was used to the routine and almost expected to be selected. Yet I had not experienced having each and every one of my family members, four of us in a row, pulled aside. Nobody else on the entire flight, a flight on which we happened to be the only people appearing to be of Middle Eastern descent, was checked. While we stood to the side and watched our fellow passengers receive friendly smiles and polite wishes for a comfortable and safe flight, we had our bodies brusquely searched with a metal detector. We watched security guards open our carry-on bags and carelessly toss around the life possessions that we had so carefully packed. I will never forget hearing the complaints of these attendants as they roughly handled my family's most precious belongings, whining to one another that our overly efficient packing made it difficult for them to do their job.

The security personnel spoke to us in a monotone, their voices revealing no trace of empathy for towards us. Clearly, they could not have known how incredibly emotionally charged this trip was for me and my family. But what shocked me was that they seemed to have forgotten that we were people just like them, that the pictures that they were flipping through documented birthdays and silly moments and first baby steps, and that we had not said or done anything that made us undeserving of the basic decency and signs of respect given to all the other passengers. Above and beyond all else, I was disturbed that the guards showed no signs of shared humanity.

We were the last passengers on the flight despite being the first in line to board. Worse, we found that all of the overhead bins were completely full. In stark contrast to our earlier demeanor, my family was now far from silent and passively depressed. We had managed to contain our irritation during the security check, retaining an air of docility to avoid trouble. Once that process was completed and we were confirmed "normal" and "safe," the emptiness in the air that hung over my family during our earlier spell of melancholy was replaced with exchanges of endless complaints. I felt insulted, degraded, and shocked at how absolutely blatantly unfair and biased the whole procedure was. Though I had been previously subjected to the racial prejudice built into airport security following September 11, I was amazed at the dehumanization of this particular operation. Before this flight, I was able to tolerate some amount of discrimination, including some extra stops at security check-points. My annoyances at these extra stops had previously been further tempered by the heightened sense of safety that they provided me with. Yet the unabashed absurdity of this particular experience opened my eyes to the flaws in the "security" system. For all the humiliation my family had to bear, I did not feel any safer.

The pain and frustration I felt was not all for naught. This experience has played a significant role in my development as a person, as a citizen of this country and this earth. While I have always spoken out against intolerance and hate, this very personal encounter made terms such as "racial profiling" come to life. It fostered an elevated and unique understanding of what these abstract concepts truly mean. I experienced firsthand the effects that it had on my psyche. As someone who now finds herself on a path leading to civil rights and social justice law, this deeper understanding has had and will continue to have an invaluable impact on how I approach matters such as racial profiling, bias incidents, and other discriminatory actions.

Yet it would be misleading to label this particular experience as the main reason for my involvement in civil rights. My interest in these issues has been developing and evolving within me for quite some time. Being of Indian descent, I have always been aware of the tensions between Hindus and Muslims in my country of heritage. The history of these tensions has deep roots, largely stemming from memories of the bloody division of the country into Hindu-majority India and Muslim-majority Pakistan in 1947. The genocidal levels of atrocity and suffering committed on all sides remain ingrained in many people's memories, and these stories of personal suffering, significant but only portraying a sliver of reality, have been passed down throughout generations. In this manner, individuals from each religion are taught that their community has committed no transgression and has been wrongly victimized. These over-simplifications and the endless cycle of vengeful hate that result have been particularly heightened in recent years with the conflict between India and Pakistan over the territory of Kashmir. I have seen even the most meek and kind of people become angry, frustrated, and downright hostile when this piece of land enters the discussion, again placing the burdens of fault on the "other" side.

In addition to growing up immersed in this environment of narrow-minded blame and hate, I have also learned about the shameful days of slavery and Jim Crow in America through my school classes. I learned that Jim Crow refers to the laws and regulations in the American

South during the early twentieth century that sought to prevent African Americans from achieving economic, political, and cultural power and equality with whites. Essentially, they functioned as a way to continue oppressing African Americans in light of the elimination of legal slavery. In these cases and many others, the common themes of blind anger, hate and division, and the endless cycle of revenge have always boggled my mind. My college education has only served to enhance and bring out these pre-existing sensitivities. Beyond learning how prejudice and discrimination lead society to hinder the progress of certain groups, my education here at Berkeley has provided me with invaluable insight into my own biases and stereotyping. Even though I have learned from many teachers, there was one class my freshman year that opened my eyes to the stunning reality that I was not immune to the same types of prejudice and stereotyping that I condemn in others. Learning that even I, someone who had spent her entire life preaching open-mindedness to others, had my own prejudices was a life-altering experiencing that crushed my deterministic view of hate. So for example, though I had always recognized the vices of passing judgment on others based on their race, the material that I was exposed to in that class revealed to me that I had several uninformed beliefs about the abilities and reasons for struggle faced by minorities such as African Americans and Latinos. Because I did not previously comprehend or grasp the enormous influence of social structure and historical events on creating the relative differences in success between these "underrepresented" minority groups and Asian Americans, I held the more traditionally ignorant view that these disparities reflected cultural differences among racial groups. Failing to see these environmental obstacles made me more prone to advocate "self-help" methods to overcome their difficulties, methods that I now view as perpetuating racial stratification in American society.

Moreover, my classes opened my mind, teaching me concepts like institutional racism. I have new understanding of discrimination in society and a burning desire to do something about it. As a result, I have sought to both challenge my own ways of looking at and dealing with people in daily life, pushing beyond my stereotypes and expectations to look at them as individuals, and to teach others to do the same.

In accomplishing the goal of teaching others what I have learned from my own experiences, both in and out of the classroom, I have found that my airport experience holds significant weight and importance. It has enabled me to speak more powerfully and authoritatively on an issue that would otherwise amount to little more than textbook knowledge. Recounting this incident to anyone I may encounter, complete with details and emotions, enables people to empathize. It is an effective form of altering mindset, attitude, and behavior. My story humanizes discussions, debates, and ideas, and consequently provides impetus for genuine change in the way we treat one another and function as a world community. I have found that the shock factor elicited by this sort of incident has lasting power. By breathing life into the elusive mention of "post-9/11 backlash," people are able to get a taste of what those words mean. Attaching a familiar face and personality to the victim enables those I speak with to recognize just how ridiculous and baseless such stereotyping is.

Beyond immediate acquaintances and friends, I have sought to share this story with others in order to impact as many people as possible. My airport experience has also enabled me to do more effective and illustrative work for the Racial Justice Advisory Board. This group was housed at the Young Women's Christian Association (YWCA) of Berkeley, and was composed of approximately ten Berkeley students. Its purpose was to conceive of and implement a local grassroots campaign that somehow promoted racial justice in the community. Our board chose to host a series of workshops aimed at informing Bay Area high school students about various racial justice issues including immigration, gentrification, and hate crimes/media bias. The group also works towards empowering the students to work towards a solution. I developed and presented information on hate crimes and media bias. By sharing my story about the airport security checkpoint, I had the unique ability to relate to these students in a way that would otherwise be impossible. As I spoke about what happened to me that day, I could see the kids nodding their heads, somber expressions forming upon their faces. More importantly, my story made them willing to share their own experiences with prejudice, fostering classroom discussions that brought previously suppressed issues to the surface. Although we discussed theories, concepts, and ideas, I found that my seemingly simple contribution of this story was one of the most effective tools used during the entire session. In enabling these young students to candidly and thoroughly explore issues of bias, I saw that they were able to internalize these problems on a deeper level and more fully empower themselves to alter the stereotypes of themselves and others around them.

While it is impossible to cleanse ourselves of our inherent biases, the key to creating a more welcoming local, national, and global community is for all of us to recognize our own prejudices and to keep a check on them. Changing negative attitudes and beliefs requires acknowledging differences between cultures while recognizing that individuals should not be judged by their group identity. Transformations will occur when every person gives up his deterministic view of hate and bias, and instead expends his energies on understanding others. I look forward to a day when people open their ears and hearts rather than simply pointing fingers. That is a day that will validate the worth of my airport experience, a day that will ease the growing pains incalculably.

Sam Keninger

It was nighttime in Kazakhstan and I was watching a Brazilian soap opera. Soap operas are great for learning new languages because the dialogue is often slow, simple, and dramatic. I had been in the country for three months, had completed the Peace Corps training program, and was finally placed at a worksite. I left the room at a commercial break to start boiling water for my supper. When I came back to the living room, CNN was broadcasting in perfect English – a first for Kazakhstan. At first I thought it was a movie; perhaps I had accidentally changed the channel.

For the next six hours I stayed in my apartment and watched the events unfold. I sat in disbelief, horror and amazement. I was curious about what lay ahead. I made frantic phone calls to ensure my loved ones weren't near the attacks. I prayed.

I am still amazed by how quickly I learned of the events. I had just moved from a house where water was drawn from a well and the restroom was a five-minute walk past the garden, yet somehow lived CNN found its way into my living room.

When I finally made it to bed, I realized that I was twelve time zones away from home in a predominantly Muslim country. I was half a world away but close to the epicenter of what was to come.

Kazakhstan is geographically one of the largest countries in the world, yet hardly anyone in America can locate it on a map. About four times the size of Texas, this former Soviet Republic nestles south of Russia and to the northwest of China. The country is a great flat steppe bordered by enormous, lush mountains. Kazakhstan is one of the least densely populated countries, yet it is rich in oil and natural resources. Western firms, like Chevron Texaco, are developing a significant presence in Kazakhstan. It is the land where Europe meets Asia, a place that has been ruled by a variety of empires, from Genghis Khan, to the Ottomans, to the Russians. In the 20th century, Stalin decided that Kazakhstan was a good place to dump full groupings of what he termed "undesirable ethnicities." There are still villages where German is the common language and Korean salads have integrated into everyone's diet.

After Stalin, Khrushchev flooded the region with native Russian farmers in his efforts to turn the steppe into self-sufficient wheat farms during the Virgin Lands Campaigns. In all, Kazakhstan is the home of over 150 different ethnicities. Many countries have negative experiences with such diversity. This one, having been beaten down century after century, has no choice but to accept it.

The Kazak people, who make up half the country, descend from the clans that stayed behind after Genghis Khan's conquest. They have Asian features, not Middle-Eastern, speak a language similar to Turkish, and are predominately Muslim. Soviet rule moderated the faith. Russian vodka has assimilated into all forms of life, but the faith is still alive and well for most in Kazakhstan. There has been a resurgence of mosques being built after independence in the early nineties, but most of the practices never really left. The Kazaks are a peaceful group. Cultural diversity, although thrust upon this country over the ages, thrives and makes up a dynamic, open culture. As many of the former Soviet countries continue to struggle to define themselves, Kazakhstan, with its diverse population, has been a model of peaceful coexistence.

While September 11 will remain in my head forever, September 12 remains in my heart. One of my dearest friends in Kazakhstan, Tleubek, whose family I lived with for the first couple of months, woke me up with a phone call, offering me permanent residence, or cash, if I wanted to fly home. My inbox had over fifty messages. Friends in America wanted to know that I was safe. Many used the occasion to say, "I love you." I quickly spammed half of America expressing that I felt safer than most of them.

My new neighbors dropped by before I left for work to offer condolences and support. Everyone who knew me in Kazakhstan reached out. This was the first day Kazakhstan felt like home.

When I arrived at work there was a queue of people wanting to see me. I sat in my office that morning and met with about 30 individuals. Most of my visitors were former clients, or tenants from the same office building. There were also a few strangers who simply needed to speak with an American. People brought food and gifts. The local government sent an officer with an official statement of condolence. The local mosque sent one of its leaders to give me a tibiteca, a traditional Kazak hat. He invited me to the mosque for a prayer session. By the end of the morning, my desk had no room for another bouquet of flowers.

36

The warmth I received from the U.S. and from my new home was comforting, but during that same time I inherited some unwanted diplomatic responsibilities. It had only been fifteen hours since the first plane hit and the Muslim world already felt the need to defend itself. Of the people I met with that morning, most of them had the same message:

1) I hope you and your family are okay.

2) Let me know how I can help you during this time.

3) Please know that Muslims are peaceful people and not terrorists.

I remember hugging a complete stranger who was in tears pleading with me to share this side of Central Asia with the rest of America. I remember person after person coming into that office so humiliated with the newfound association with the terrorists that they would do anything to personally make it up to me. And I remember my feelings of love and comfort being overtaken that afternoon by a feeling of pity. I wondered why they felt a need to explain such things. I was not prepared to represent my country. How could I offer appropriate answers when there was so much taking place in America that I did not understand?

I went home after an exhausting day. I declined the dinner invitations and shut off my phone. I read news on the internet and scoured through the local papers to see how September 11 was portrayed. I saw the reoccurrence of the words "Muslim Extremists" in both local and American media. I decided to read my morning's email more closely. I did not see the same messages when I read the emails a second time. What I read initially was loving and only slightly naive. When I read them again, I saw bigotry. These messages were from loved ones who could not relate to my experience, but it was difficult to justify quotes like "stay away from Muslims" and "consider purchasing a weapon."

Nearly every Peace Corps Volunteer is filled with a longing to change the world. Before going to bed that night, I reconfirmed my personal mission to show Americans that the majority of Central Asians are enlightened sympathizers and to show the people of Kazakhstan that not all Americans are ignorant fools.

This mission got stronger as America prepared to go after the Taliban. I personally felt safe even with the invasion of Afghanistan, primarily because the Tian Shan Mountains, along the southern border of

Kazakhstan, are enormous. Neither battle spillovers nor refugees were a real concern in Kazakhstan, but perceptions on both sides intensified as American troops began entering the region. I didn't know how to manage either side. I was confused about how Americans would react, largely because I could not relate to America in its post September 11 state. I needed to form an opinion. Of course I wasn't anti-Muslim. And I wasn't ready to denounce my U.S. citizenship. During that time, pressures felt so great that these two options appeared mutually exclusive, even though nothing is ever this black and white.

Less than two weeks after September 11 and amidst the US buildup in Central Asia, Pope John Paul II was scheduled to visit Kazakhstan in a nearby city. This was one of the few times the pontiff ever visited a Muslim country. The meeting was scheduled long before the events of September 11, but the visit could not be timelier.

Having grown up Catholic, and considering the world's current state, nothing could have kept me away from the Pope's public mass. Unfortunately, Peace Corps had initiated "standfast," a version of house arrest that kept all volunteers at their sites until the events of the pending war unfolded. I thought about sneaking out of town and hopping on the fifteen-hour train ride without telling Peace Corps headquarters or the State Department, but I decided against that. Luckily, pulling the religion card worked and I was allowed to go.

The privilege came with its own hassles. I was briefed by security experts at the American consulate and had to check in every other hour with a Peace Corps employee. I was given advice such as: "Try your best to stay in groups of ethnic Russians so you blend in."

The mass Pope John Paul II conducted was magical. He managed the crowd of 50,000 despite his advanced stage of Parkinson's disease. During his homily he said, "The Muslim sage Abai Kunanbai, an authoritative representative of Kazak culture, spoke from a great heart when he said: "Precisely because we worship God fully and have faith in him, we have no right to claim that we must force others to believe in him and worship him . . . We must not let what has happened [on September 11] lead to a deepening of divisions . . . I invite both Christians and Muslims to raise an intense prayer to the one Almighty God, whose children we all are." He also called on all nations to resolve these issues peacefully. The crowd was peaceful and quiet. I recalled the advice given to me by the consulate to stay away from people who looked Muslim. That was simply impossible. More than half of the people there were native Kazaks. The rest were mainly Orthodox Christians, which is even more remarkable because the Russian Orthodox Church did not have a good relationship with this Pope. The locals attended with respect, stayed during the entire long service, and enthusiastically rushed to see the Popemobile go by. I was proud of the Pope's message and the way my host country represented itself that day. For the first time in a couple of weeks, I had heard a message that made sense and that could be used to bridge the gap between America and Kazakhstan.

I returned from my trip to Astana without incident, but the Pope's visit didn't cure my discontent. In the days ahead, I began hearing stories from the U.S. that sickened me even further. Emails about discrimination and retaliatory violence came in every day. My mother's neighbors complained because her house did not have an American flag. I didn't understand and was too far away to have a perspective, leaving me confused.

Stories of discrimination in America were published and embellished in Kazakhstan newspapers every day. I was constantly asked why Americans were reacting this way. People around me also continued to dispute the war. I decided the best way to make it through my two years there was to simply agree with the Kazakhstan masses and reject U.S. aggression. I justified it to myself by saying this approach was consistent with the Pope's call for peace. But in addition to denouncing a war, which is not necessarily unpatriotic, I changed my rhetoric about America. When people asked me about America, I no longer discussed its virtues. In fact, in most accounts I criticized the US and reassured locals how lucky they were to live in Kazakhstan.

Worries about the war spilling into Kazakhstan eased and Peace Corps lifted its standfast near the end of 2001. I used the opportunity to visit Tleubek, the man who took me into his home when I arrived. We hadn't talked since his call on September 12.

Tleubek is a native Kazak and Muslim. Many of his aunts and uncles were killed during Stalin's reign by being forced to give up their nomadic ways and take up collectivized farming, a practice they knew nothing about.

Tleubek spent four years fighting for the Soviet army against other Muslims in Afghanistan. He now admits his strong opposition to that war, during which he lost an eye. Even though he was not comfortable talking about that part of his life, he once sadly revealed to me that he had probably killed 15 to 20 people.

Tleubek has two sons. In 2001 they were 12 and 14 years old. Neither child is allowed to mention war. When the youngest mentioned he wanted to be a General. Tleubek calmly replied, "No son of mine will go to war. You're going to be a businessman."

Having dealt with questions of American foreign policy with most people I encountered and knowing Tleubek's history in Afghanistan, I wanted to be clear that I did not support the war. I thought this was what he wanted to hear. His opinion mattered a lot to me.

I wish I could say that Tleubek was proud of me. He was not. He was surprised at my anti-war position, and was shocked to hear my criticism of the US. He argued that America, in order to protect itself, needed to expunge the Taliban and find Bin Laden immediately. Despite his general opposition to war, he felt a US invasion of Afghanistan was necessary. He also told me that the assumption that Muslims would not support an American attack on the Taliban was just as wrong and shortsighted as assuming that all Muslims are terrorists.

I left my weekend at Tleubek's feeling relieved that America's attacks wouldn't drive a stake through our friendship. He could still distinguish between Soviet imperialism and American defense. Tleubek was the first to show me that my quest to be fair and impartial was neglecting an important element of consideration – my own country. Unfortunately, this wisdom didn't sink in until I returned to the States.

For the next year and a half I remained overly critical of the U.S. This seemed easy on the onset of the Iraqi invasion. The same people who comforted me after September 11 were wondering how the U.S. could justify another war under the guise of fighting terrorism. I couldn't get into a taxi without being pressed to take a position on the war. As always, I comforted the people of Kazakhstan by bashing the U.S.

On the day Iraq was invaded, I sat across a park full of young men who gathered in protest chanting "Jihad." It was scary to see, but it made perfect sense. Kazakhstan, the most open culture I'd ever seen, had come to this. It was hard not to think things would have been different if America reacted to September 11 differently.

The world had changed and so had I, both in unexpected ways. Soon my service in Kazakhstan was completed and I needed to think about returning to the U.S. I had not been home for over two years. While I wanted to see my family and friends again, part of me wasn't ready to go back.

I naively felt everyone in America was blindly supporting an Iraq invasion. I cringed at the thought of seeing my mom's street forcefully lined with flags. And I didn't want to answer the ignorant questions about various prejudices and stereotypes. Nevertheless, I was set to return to the U.S. on July 4, 2003 — America's Independence Day.

My flight back to Chicago was uneventful. When I went through customs, the official greeted me with the warmest "Welcome Home" I have ever received. That night I enjoyed wonderful food with great customer service, a concept that I had long forgotten. I immediately remembered the little things that make the U.S. a great place to live, conversations with strangers, people watching baseball games in the bar, senior citizens with smiles on their faces. As the sun went down I walked over to Navy Pier to watch fireworks. Along the way the Wrigley Building was draped in the largest flag I have ever seen. It gave me goose bumps. I was happy to see it despite my fears and opinions about my country. Amidst all my excitement in coming back I lost sight of all the good that America has to offer. I was home and it felt great.

I was surprised to come home to an America that was much more open then I envisioned. People eagerly wanted to hear my account and were sympathetic. Through time I began to better understand America after September 11. In Kazakhstan, I experienced something that most Americans weren't fortunate enough to see, but I missed out on an important time in my country's evolution.

In this period of my life, I saw just how complex the world is. CNN can zip half way around the world and find its way into the barren Kazakhstan Steppe, creating the illusion of infinite exposure to the world. But our exposure is limited. No one can ever see all sides to a situation. To see all sides, we have to talk to one another and that is something CNN can not provide.

I'm often reminded of the man from the local mosque who simply invited me to attend a prayer session with him, or the Pope's call for ecumenism, or Tleubek's wisdom of not seeing the world in black and white. These men taught me that we must stay open, especially during times of crises. Ironically, it is during such times that people stop talking and listening. We must not allow that to happen, whether our home is in the US or in Kazakhstan or anywhere else in between.

One American's Journey in the Wake of Sept. 11

Caroline LeFeber

Middlebury, Vermont, 2001

I hit the snooze a few too many times on the morning of the eleventh, and didn't even have time for my usual quick muffin. I rushed to my 9:30 painting class only to find the room half empty – perhaps I wasn't late after all? But my watch said I was. The professor turned a tragic face my way. "I don't think we can hold class today, considering the… circumstances." The circumstances? My confusion far greater than my dread, I wandered away from Middlebury's art department, too embarrassed to question him further.

Outside on the sunny Vermont lawn I saw groups of people engaged in intense conversation, wandering aimlessly or sitting on the grass. No one was holding class, it seemed. I joined a friend of mine on the lawn, a petite economics student from India who was sitting alone. "What happened? I just woke up." "A plane crashed into the World Trade Center, in New York," she replied, as if that should have explained everything. It didn't, not yet – I didn't understand. Was it an accident? Is that an important building? I'd only been to New York once, and the most memorable attraction had been that street lined with shoe stores. "Just come with me, you'll see," and she grabbed my arm and took me to the television in the cafeteria's lounge. There, straining to see through the crowd of hushed college students, I saw, over and over again, not one but two commercial planes destroying those monumental towers. I silently tried to assimilate the scale of the explosion, incomparable to anything any of us already carried in our memories or imaginations. The other faces in our little crowd looked much like mine… frantic denial becoming numb shock. Perhaps it took us so long to become horrified because we'd seen it all before in Hollywood special effects? But we slowly began to understand. And then several of us began to sob as we realized that those little dots falling in the fuzzy image were people, panicking in the flames and jumping to their deaths.

I counted my family members and friends in my mind, assuring myself that they were safe. My sister was at home in Wisconsin, my father at work, my mother in Chicago for a conference. Would the terrorists care about the Midwest, or Vermont? Probably not, but still my world seemed somehow more vulnerable, and the open sky more sinister.

I took my lunch outside and joined a small circle of my international friends, all gathered on the lawn in what would have been a laughing late-summer laze any other time. A freshman from Jordan sat with his too-pale face clenched in his hands. He was the first to think of the aftermath of the disaster, as the rest of us were just trying to understand that it had happened. "Do you even realize what this means?" No, we didn't. "They'll say it's us," he whispered, "even if it isn't true, they'll blame it on the Arabs, and we'll all pay for it. The whole world will change." He said that the Middle East is America's new Russia, the new Evil Opponent, and that the Bush administration will capitalize on this disaster to lead a grief-stricken and easily manipulated USA down the patriotic road to war. "Your government was just waiting for something like this so that they can wage war against us. It's a war they've always wanted but couldn't justify until now. We won't be welcome in your country anymore," he said. He looked around him at the sunny Vermont landscape as if it were already hostile to him, already judging him by his race and religion. But we were too overwhelmed to think about that yet.

By the end of the day, I had met several people who had no word from family in the city. I tried to be comforting, but what could I say? "I understand"? How could I understand something like the limbo of New York City that day, with tragedy everywhere and no phones to contact lost relatives? In the end, some of those lost family members were safe, at an appointment or late to work on the only day that really mattered, but those small, arbitrary miracles were few.

Those who lost someone mourned deeply. The rest of us, though, mourned the death of our fairy tale, our mythical invincibility, our already tenuous tolerance, our peace. America, land of safety, law, democracy, freedom; we have always felt special, apart, different. Until September, there hadn't been a glimpse of war on our shores since Pearl Harbor, so we forgot that it was ever possible. In the midst of an increasingly chaotic world, we Americans were brought up with a sense of wellbeing. We could watch international horrors on the nightly news and keep the misery at arm's length, glad to be comfortable in our great nation. But it isn't so easy anymore.

There was a beautiful unity that came out of the disaster. People all over the world felt like New Yorkers, and New Yorkers felt like a single bereaved family. "God Bless America" rang across the nation. Policemen and firemen were hailed as heroes, and we felt like a strong country that meant something, rather than just a place to freely pursue an individual dream of monetary success. The world mourned with us.

But there were casualties of this grief-stricken unity, too. We could have become constructive with our sorrow, but there was no one to tell us how; so, powerful in grief, the nation became powerful, too, in hatred. Our unity became against something, and not just against those individuals who caused the tragedy of the 11th.

A friend of mine from the Dominican Republic was pushed back off of the subway as he tried to board, sneering racial epithets thrust in his face. They thought he was Middle Eastern because he's about the right, or perhaps wrong, color. An Indian family in Dallas had eggs thrown at them in a supermarket by people who thought a sari and a burka were the same thing. A Pakistani couple running an inn in New York state hastily put flags in the windows and bought hotel key cards with stars and stripes lest their business suffer.

Many ethnic groups put American flags up in their homes and businesses to say, "We're Americans too! We're also victims of this tragedy, not perpetrators. Don't hate us!"

The prejudice and distrust were made official, too. Marriages were parted because of impossible paperwork, the now unachievable visa. A fiancé left in China until further notice, a son left in Ecuador, a ministry student from New Zealand who can't return home to her American husband, all in name of national safety, and courtesy of Homeland Security.

Lost liberties for the purpose of fighting terrorism. Who can argue against fighting terrorists? And yet, what is it we would supposedly defend and even spread abroad to that new despised "infidel" if we don't even have it at home? Many of us began to feel ashamed and even to despise our country for the hatred and prejudice that now abounded here.

We college students in Vermont were largely spared the backlash, except for one instance when someone defaced the Islamic Club's posters. As a result the student body came together to support our Middle Eastern students, listening to their calls for prayer throughout the campus on loudspeakers, and fasting with them on Ramadan. Fortunately, our world on campus was small enough that we could combat prejudice simply by getting to know each other better. In the greater world, this is much harder.

Salvador da Bahia, Brazil, 2003:

When I left Vermont to spend a year abroad in South America, I realized the full global extent of Sept. 11th and its aftermath. I soon wished I had a badge: "Please don't blame me for my country's foreign policy." For many people, any American is a representative of our economic and cultural empire, and thus at fault for the entire world's unfairness. The Latin American presses, often so censored in reporting their local and national news, are perhaps freer than ours to criticize and hate our country. And criticize us they do. I felt the glares, heard the muttering, sometimes too loud. "Gringa, go home to your war," they told me.

Feeling ashamed of the United States was not new to me, though now it felt more immediate. I had first learned to despise my America in 1998, the summer before eleventh grade, when I went to Argentina with American Field Service. The young Argentineans loved Coca-Cola and Hollywood, but felt an enduring resentment towards the American people and government. During the festival celebrating San Juan and San Pedro, high school students in Gualeguaychú, Argentina, burned huge plaster figures in order to represent both the destruction of what they hate and the elevation of what they love. One group of students was burning an indigenous symbol to honor the dead natives of their land. Another group burned a huge American Uncle Sam to represent their hatred of American imperialism, although out of some distant respect they kept the flames away from the American flag.

Those sixteen-year-olds were much more aware than I of the effects of my country's foreign policy and economic grip on the world, and I learned many things there that I was never taught in history class back home in Wisconsin. I soon decided, with adolescent zeal, that I wasn't going to represent my country anymore. I returned from Argentina and shed old friends for new ones, learned about the Mexican south side of Milwaukee, befriended the Guatemalan janitor at my high school, learned to dance salsa, and spoke Spanish as much as possible. When I went to college, I made friends with mostly international students, and I was gratified to hear from my new international and Hispanic friends that I wasn't American, that I was an honorary foreigner.

When I arrived in Brazil in the spring of 2003, the war in Iraq was starting, and the entire world's sympathy for America — which could have been used to build a worldwide unity to reflect our nation's new unity — was lost and forgotten, giving way to anger against the North American bully.

What did it mean to be an American in Salvador da Bahia, Brazil, during that time? My host mother warned me when I arrived that I had to be very careful whom I trusted. "I've told the doorman that you're my niece from São Paulo," she said. "Don't tell anyone outside the university where you're from. It wouldn't do if people thought I had an American in my home," she warned. "They might think I was aiding a terrorist or a spy."

So on my first day out the door, I dutifully closed my mouth when passing the doorman, so he couldn't hear that I was foreign. The man taking fares on the bus asked me where I was from, and I said "Argentina." You can take a bus from Argentina to Brazil, and many had done so, looking for work. I even had a Spanish accent on my Portuguese. He accepted it and smiled.

But on the street, even without speaking a word of English, I was told: "Sua branca, volte prà sua terra, aqui não queremos guerra não." (Whitey, go back to your land. We don't want war here.) A homeless man sat down next to me at the beach, his stench making me nauseous, his eyes close to mine. "Do you know why I'm poor?" he asked. "Because you're rich. You're rich and white and you're American. That's why I'm poor. Because you take everything!"

On the beach, in the clubs, in stores I was asked for money, and men flirted with me hoping to gain something, saying "you're American, you're rich, I love you, marry me, buy this!" An ice-cream vendor winked at me and offered a third flavor that I hadn't paid for, if I would give him my number or meet him after his shift. I was faced with these opportunistic men everywhere I went.

In a clothing store, I overheard two salespeople giggling about how they were going to charge that stupid American twice the price of the shirt. They reasoned that I could surely afford it, and even owed it to them. I came out of the dressing room and told them in almost-flawless

Portuguese that I was Argentinean, had just moved here, and was low on cash. Shame-faced, they gave me a discount. I wasn't happy with lying, but I had never been discriminated against until I went to Salvador, and it was an ugly feeling to be despised.

I walked into a pharmacy, a little hole in the wall, on a Sunday evening. After a few moments navigating the shelves, I brought some toothpaste up to the front. I didn't have the correct change and, as often happens, the man behind the counter had no change at all, so I had to pay with my American credit card. He said, "You're American, are you? Gringa?"

"Yes," I replied.

He tried some English on me, "Hello, how are you?" And then in Portuguese said, "So you want to live here, do you. It's better. We don't fight wars in Brazil; we don't kill people." I didn't say anything, too tired to explain to him that I am not affiliated with politics in any way and am not a terrorist, just a simple American college student trying to learn about the world. "It's cheap for you here, too. You should buy something else while you're here. Some sunscreen?" He held up a strange perfume, and a toothbrush, and gave me a hostile glance.

"No thank you, this is all I need," I said.

"Eh." He fiddled with the calculator a minute. "The total is only two dollars and 43 cents. That's nothing, right? You could buy my whole store, couldn't you? Set me up for retirement? Put my kids through college?"

I took the receipt and left.

There were a few Brazilians who reacted otherwise, idealizing me as the fine and sophisticated product of a "first-world" nation. The resulting feeling was just as awkward and hateful to me as being seen with contempt. My linguistics professor wouldn't stop staring. She was a lonely older woman, longing to travel, longing to be truly "cultured," and I was the first American to take her class. "The education there is so much better," she told my classmates, "You could all learn from this girl. Try to be like her." After that I found it almost impossible to gain the confidence of my classmates, many of whom were women in their early 30s struggling to be independent, tougher and much more experienced than I.

In my other classes at the university, the Universidade Católica, I introduced myself as the American exchange student in class and was met with closed and hostile faces. I had to prove to them over the next few months that I was not the terrible, greedy, war-hungry, privileged and ignorant fool that they thought I might be. I had to prove over and over again, to students and professors both, that I was in their country because of an honest love of diverse cultures and languages, and that I was willing to pull my weight. And once I earned their trust and friendship, I was told again, just as I had been in Argentina and Vermont, "We understand now that you're not typical, that you're not defined by your country. You're special, not American."

"We're glad that you don't support that war," they added, "it was completely unfounded, you understand, since in so many ways America had really been asking for a terrorist attack for years, because of its actions. We're glad you understand, glad you're different." But wait. How could I agree with that? Was I really supposed to believe that my country deserved such a terrible thing? And was I supposed to be proud, too, of denouncing and even publicly denying my origins? Did it somehow prove that I was open-minded and worldly? That didn't seem right.

Although it had pleased me in the past, that day for the first time I was deeply bothered by the label, "different." Something inside me finally rebelled. I didn't want to lie anymore in the face of discrimination abroad, or agree when my peers condemned my country. I realized then that the USA is me, too, and I couldn't seek happiness any longer in being accepted by others as an exception to some American rule. I had to prove to the world that Americans could be different than the stereotype, not that I was different from an American.

I knew they wouldn't understand, but I wanted to tell my new friends: "No, I'm not different. There are things that I love about my country and things that I deeply despise, but no matter what, I was born and raised there, and I am an American." I thought of all the people I knew at home and how wonderful they are, and I resented my frequent denial of any connection to my home.

After that moment I started to reflect more than I ever had about my place in the world. I realized that there was much to criticize and much to love about every country. America can be ignorant and ethnocentric, but it is also, among many other things, the birthplace of Jazz, a beautiful wide land rich with diversity and full of talented and thoughtful people. And as much as I have always loved Latin America for its rich cultures, beautiful music, wonderful people and fascinating literature, there are things I disagree with there, too, such as certain views of gender or individuality.

My truce with the U.S.A. was difficult, because hatred is easier than understanding and I was ashamed of what my country had done over the years in Latin America and other less wealthy regions. But I had been wrong to think that "you're an honorary foreigner" was a compliment. I'm not alone here in my ideals; there are many other Americans too who, like me, seek to be more tolerant of difference and more knowledgeable about the world. I wanted to reply finally to those comments from all of my international friends, "thank you for thinking that I'm worthy of being of your culture – Dominican, Indian, Kenyan, Brazilian – but realize that I am not who I am 'despite' my upbringing and citizenship, but rather I am who I am and that is all a part of me." Any show of American patriotism would have had me viewed as closed-minded among my liberal and foreign friends. But can I not love many things that my country stands for, and work to better the rest? Am I not a product of my place, and an active member of my society?

I don't agree with a lot of what America has done; I feel that my country is shirking many of the responsibilities that come with power, and allowing ignorance to work together with greed in its foreign affairs. I hate the bigotry that has ensued in the wake of September 11th; it angers me and shames me and frightens me. But I also don't agree with the stereo-typed definition of America that claims that any patriotism represents the imperialistic, condescending attitude that the world expects of Americans, the view that "the world is our back yard." I don't agree that the only patriotism that exists is that superficial "patriotism" of American-flag-ridden souvenirs and advertising campaigns which are, more simply, capitalism at its worst and most ironic. In a way, I think, the flag has been stolen from us over time; it has been cheapened on match-boxes and napkins, and has come to represent a warlike and ignorant pride rather than being a symbol for unity, tolerance, freedoms, and responsibilities.

So what should we do? We Americans who are frustrated with the way things are need to stop denying our citizenship and take part in the solution instead. I can leave my country in protest and lie about my origins, but shouldn't I be bailing water, instead of jumping ship just because the U.S. is the villain of the hour? That's what it means to be a part of something. We need to accept our responsibilities and better our country; we need to be active in our society and government, to change the things that we disagree with rather than just complaining about them.

If my little Vermont liberal arts college could survive those events with a community intact, then perhaps we can learn from that. That widely diverse college community stayed afloat because people tried to get to know and understand each other. We need to try to do that on a bigger scale as well. We should make it a priority for every American to travel the world, meet people and talk. Live together, eat together. We need to explain to the world that the open-minded and forward-thinking American is not the exception. And we need to listen, too. We need to have dialogues and get to know each other as humans and not as stereotypes.

I went back to Brazil this summer, and had a far different experience than before, one that gave me a lot of hope. I wandered with my host mother deep into the interior of Bahia. We stopped and gave clothing and food to indigent farmers. As I handed cookies to some bashful, barely-clad girls I said "hello" to them, in English, and asked if they wanted to learn that word. But they didn't understand what it meant to speak another language. It didn't mean anything to those girls that I was American – I had green eyes and white skin, and cookies. That was fascinating, and that was all. Beyond that, I was just a person, unlabeled, unjudged, proven only by my actions. I was seen as just a human being, and welcome to come in and have some of their coffee even if it was their last cup.

Practicing Human Rights After 9/11:
A Correspondence

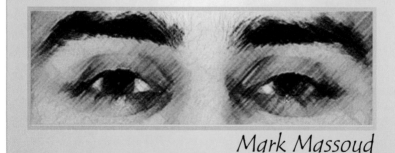

Mark Massoud

February 16, 2002

Dear Ramzi,

I write you this note from an airplane seven miles above American soil. I fear that as an Arab like me, you understand all too closely my story.

Sometimes, when I'm traveling on an airplane, I cry — tears of joy because I'm going somewhere new or because I'm going somewhere familiar to see old friends. I love to travel because I learn about new places and cultures, and because I have the opportunity to visit friends and family who live far away.

Today, however, I sobbed for a different reason. Once again, at the airport, I was seized, searched, and detained. Once again, I found myself waiting at the boarding gate, shoeless, bags open, my arms extended in the air as if being crucified, while an airport employee with a magic wand and a hand closely behind it felt each crevice of my body — another painful and humiliating experience.

When can I find solace, my friend? If an airport security gate agent sees my driver's license or passport, then I am subject to a security search. I am a 25-year old Arab-looking man, with an Arabic-sounding name, and I was born in Sudan. I think the security translation of this information is "randomly searchable."

Arriving at the airport was fine. I made it through the first security checkpoint hassle-free. When I arrived at the gate and showed my boarding pass and my identification, I was asked to step aside for a further "security check." I felt humiliated. Not because this was the first time I lost my privacy at an airport. Not because this was the second time, or the third, fourth, or fifth. I have been searched on every trip I have taken since October 2001.

The airport employees opened my bags and rummaged through my life — their hands scavenging like hungry rats in a pantry. They saw where I keep my Efferdent cleaner for my retainer. They saw where I keep a condom. They saw my wooden Virgin Mary icon that I bought from a monastery in western Greece. They pierced into my life, and, when they were sufficiently armed with the knowledge of my most intimate details, they set me free. I put on my shoes, and helped them re-pack my bags. Though I was one of the first to get to the gate, I was one of the last to board the plane. When I walked onto the plane, most passengers were seated, seatbelts fastened. They had waited patiently. They had seen me searched. They had walked past me. Some had turned their heads to look twice to see me, my shoes near me, my bags opened, my clothes and toiletries strewn around like entrails on an operating table.

Why am I so sad, my friend? Why do I feel so much pain? News reports claim that people all across America are subject to such strict scrutiny. I know that I am not alone. I know that these are safety procedures. Intuitively I know I should not feel threatened or hurt by these measures. But I am subject to them so often — more often than my friends who do not share a similar name, who do not share a similar color. Only a few people are pulled aside to be searched during each boarding process. Why have I found myself always a member of this group?

I dream of the days when I used to travel without having to take off my shoes and without having to open my bags prior to boarding an airplane. I dream of anonymity, when people didn't stare at me, when I didn't feel humiliated.

Ramzi, my friend, when I boarded the plane, I held my head up high once again to face the passengers sitting in their seats — all of whom had watched me sitting quietly at the boarding gate, detained, shoeless, vulnerable, isolated. I will not let myself be taken down. I will not let myself be hurt. But I cannot be cold and forgetful of my experiences.

Sometimes I feel that if I am this hurt, then surely there are other Arab Americans who are hurt and angry. I worry about this anger. Is it fruitful in our current political and economic climate? Are these searches fruitful? At some moments I say yes, because I want to feel safe on an airplane. But, I just want to be a dignified human being when I'm at the airport. Why am I always singled out? My hurt swallows me.

Thank you for listening, habibi. I look forward to seeing you upon my return to California in a couple of months.

Amal wa hub (hope and love),
Mark

March 2, 2002

Dear Mark,

Thank you for your letter. Usually you are the optimist. Now I feel that I must be the one to remind you that things will get better. Arab-Americans will move past the racial stereotyping that victimize them. Of course I too have experienced some of the "random searches" – all of us in the community have.

But at least we are not Japanese living in California during the Second World War. Remember innocent people were interned in camps because of their ethnic background. And you're a law student...remember the U.S. Supreme Court case, Korematsu? That's when the Supreme Court upheld the legality of those internment camps because America was at war with Japan. Even the courts – the independent branch of government – seemed to side against civil rights. Though we are not being detained in camps, our civil liberties are being threatened each time we are detained at airports. Why do the darkest moments of history seem to rear their ugly heads in new ways? So, unless you count airport detentions, there have been no internments, no concentration camps for Arabs in the U.S. Some of my Middle Eastern friends try to pass for Italian, or Latino. It works only until they show their IDs.

Mark, you are not going to want to hear this. The searches are not going away anytime soon. Challenge yourself to change it. Raise awareness about it. And remember, you are composed of more than simply your Arab identity. There is more to my friend Mark than his Arab-ness.

Love,
Ramzi

April 9, 2002

Dear Ramzi,

Thank you for your letter. I knew that you would understand the pain and the humiliation that I experience too often at airports. I wish I didn't have to travel so much. But, as a student of human rights law, I am often on airplanes, traveling to conflict zones. My travels have taken me to far-away places to study the abuses of human rights law – South

Africa, Venezuela, Egypt, Turkey, Lebanon, and the Sudan. I never expected that as an American citizen, I would be a victim here in the U.S.

I took your advice to heart. You reminded me that my identity is composed of more than just my ethnicity. I'm not sure if this is what you meant — but on my most recent flight, I played up my gay identity. I wore a gay pride T-shirt — something I would not normally do, least of all at an airport. Clutching a teddy bear, I told the gate agent how cute her highlights were — and those black pumps, gorgeous and so easy on the heels! I'm usually more subdued. But if my Arab identity is publicized at the airport, why shouldn't my gay identity go along with it? Being gay is less threatening to a gate agent than being Arab. And you know what? It worked. She did not send me aside for a search. For the first time since September 11, I walked freely onto an airplane. I'm not sure I want to come out to gate agents just to avoid the hassle associated with TWA, Traveling While Arab, but it will have to do for now.

Amal wa hub,
Mark

May 26, 2002

Dear Mark,

How ironic that you had to be gay in order not to appear Arab! Most people assume that all Arabs are straight. We're not all Muslims either. Your parents and you are Roman Catholic. If the gate agents only knew about the film you were in, "I Exist," and how it won best documentary awards at film festivals in New York and in Italy, for its portrayal of gay Middle Easterners.

When I write to you about identity, I am reminded of when we marched together in the Arab contingent at Gay Pride in San Francisco last year. Most people smiled and clapped at our signs, "Anti-gay = Anti-Arab" and "Queer Persian and Arab Unity." Others stared at us as exotic and foreign, as if watching the cast of "Aladdin" walk by.

Do you remember the woman along the parade route who stopped clapping when she saw us and shook her head in disdain? She motioned to us as if we were allowed to be gay in public, but not Arab. I didn't know what to do, but you did. You looked her directly in the eyes and held up your fingers in a peace sign.

Knowing that our gay identities and our Arab identities are not to be separated helped us to deal with the shame we receive from Arabs for being gay and from Americans for being Arab.

Let me know how things shake out. Be in touch.

Love,

Ramzi

July 18, 2004

Dear Ramzi,

Today I have a painful story to share, of airport abuse. I thought these experiences were something of the past, but they are not. I am sorry you are the one who must read about yet another story of airport abuse. Let me give you some background. I was asked recently by the Carter Center to go to Venezuela as an international elections observer. Working for human rights with a team led by a former President who also won the Nobel Peace Prize, will be unforgettable. At one point during my work in Venezuela I found myself encircled by two mobs of protesters who wanted to file complaints with me about the mishandling of the elections by the other side. I briefed President Carter on my work. Another observer asked me to join his legal team to work on a Supreme Court case on behalf of migrant farm workers in Florida.

Unfortunately, my mistreatment at Miami International was a 180-degree turn from those dignified experiences… I sent a letter to my friend, Paco, an attorney in Miami. I have copied that letter on the next page for you to read.

Amal wa hub,

Mark

June 15, 2004

Dear Paco,

It was great to meet you in Caracas a couple of weeks ago. I'm still keeping in mind your offer to work on the migrant workers' Supreme Court case. Working on human rights issues in the U.S. is something of a dream come true. I am now in New York, fulfilling other responsibilities for a human rights organization here.

I am writing to tell you about my experience at the Miami International Airport while in transit from Caracas to New York. I was detained for about two hours, mostly at a secondary inspection area at the airport. My bags were searched thoroughly and I was interrogated by a Department of Homeland Security (DHS) official. The DHS uniforms are more militaristic in appearance than the old INS uniforms, making me feel instantaneously like some sort of prisoner of war. The agent asked me about the countries stamped in my passport, mostly the Middle Eastern or African countries. He asked me why I visited those countries, whom I met, and what they told me. I told him, for example, that I visited Cairo on a package tour with two friends for spring break in 1997 while I was on a semester-abroad in Athens, Greece; and that I have family in Lebanon. Later, he entered my passport number into a nearby computer, and in the "notes" section on the screen, he typed what I had told him, including the following, which I was able to see over his shoulder:

Pax [passenger] was at a Carter Center function in Venezuela. Pax has digital photos of President Carter....Pax studies human rights. Pax intends to work in human rights.

After entering the notes, the screen switched to a "race" screen. It had various categories: white, black, and Asian. I am not sure what he checked. He moved away so that I could not see the screen.

Of the six Carter Center observers on my flight, I was the only one detained. I look Arab. My last name is Arabic. My passport says I was born in the Sudan, and I have traveled extensively in the Middle East.

I haven't been able to sleep well since this incident. I've been waking up in the middle of the night from nightmares, mostly re-living the interrogation and humiliation. It is not fair that I was forced to share my private details with the federal government just to enter my country of citizenship. And now the DHS has an active file on me. I might think differently if every American were treated similarly. But I was singled out, and this does not seem just.

Paco, you and I both were raised in Catholic families. Both of us remain devoutly religious. After the Homeland Security agent at the airport let me go, I called my parents and told them the story. They listened and cried. These humiliating procedures, once perpetrated by a brutal Sudanese regime against my family, were the same reasons my parents left Sudan over 20 years ago and came to the U.S. as refugees. This is our cross to bear, my mother told me.

Aside from my parents, I have spoken only to you about this. I know my story is common for immigrants and non-citizens. But have these "airport detentions" been perpetrated against other U.S. citizens? I thought the 14th Amendment of the U.S. Constitution prevented these arbitrary invasions of privacy.

Cuidate,

Mark

August 15, 2004

Dear Mark,

I am not sure how to respond to your experiences in detention at the Miami airport. Despite your negative experiences over the least three years in airports, it sounds to me like there is a vision of hope here. Let me try to develop that vision, based on what you wrote to me.

It seems to me that you've done three things to counteract the prejudice and stereotypes that you've experienced. Those are, practicing, praying, and being honest to yourself. And these three everyday experiences make up your vision for a better America.

Regarding "practicing," even though you have had terrible experiences at American airports, those experiences have not stopped you from pressing for human rights. Human rights advocates in your situation are vilified at borders and treated as if they are terrorists in the making simply because they've traveled to the same countries that terrorists have traveled to. Nevertheless, you have not given up your efforts to make the world a better place for all people, including Americans. While the American Civil Liberties Union and other organizations use national legal strategies, your strategy is deeply personal. Your work reminds me that fighting stereotypes and bigotry after September 11th is not only about big legal challenges, but also about personal strategies. It's practicing these grassroots strategies, which anyone can do, that gives me hope.

Regarding "praying," it's clear that religion has played an important role in your work. Though I am not religious myself, I know that you take prayer seriously in your life. Your commitment to prayer and your admiration for Jesus Christ as a leader who helped the poor has enabled you to think clearly and positively. After all, why do you continue the work that you do, knowing the challenges that you face? Your faith has guided you on a path that allows you to see long-term. Just as things changed for the Japanese in America after World War II, so too will things eventually change for Arabs in America after September 11.

And Mark, you have been true to all parts of your identity. This openness offers hope to those of us who are gay and Arab. You are honest to yourself and about yourself. What you have done is become a real-life example of what the black feminist poet, Audre Lorde, wrote about 25 years ago:

> I find I am constantly being encouraged to pluck out some one aspect of myself and present this as the meaningful whole, eclipsing or denying the other parts of self. But this is a destructive and fragmenting way to live. My fullest concentration of energy is available to me only when I integrate all the parts of who I am, openly, allowing power from particular sources of my living to flow back and forth freely through all my different selves, without the restrictions of externally imposed definition.

The poet Lorde tells us that we are all made up of different "selves," and it is in combining them seamlessly that we gain power. You have taken your different identities — ethnic, religious, sexual — and combined them to make a difference as an advocate for human rights, in the face of challenge — whether they be mobs of angry protesters in Venezuela or Homeland Security border agents at airports in America. These three daily commitments — practicing and fighting for human rights, praying, and being honest to yourself — make you who you are today. And these commitments provide hope for those of us who challenge bigotry and stereotyping in the wake of the September 11 attacks.

I cannot wait to welcome you home with open arms.

Love, your friend,

Ramzi

Author's note: All events and persons mentioned in this essay are actual, though some names have been changed to protect privacy. Though portrayed as an exchange of letters, this essay was written entirely by the author.

63

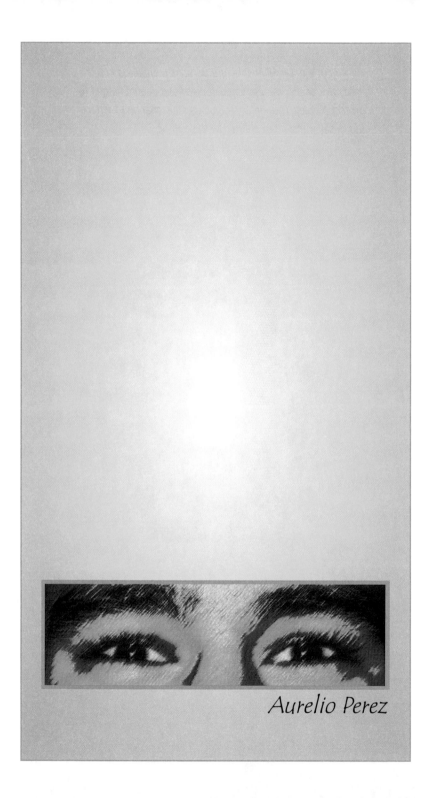

Aurelio Perez

It was September 12th, 2001, and a retired bowling alley manager from Southeastern Ohio named Ralph Leroy Hutchinson cancelled a trip that he had been planning for a couple of weeks. He remained at home, quiet.

The next morning, he loaded a rifle and a shotgun into his pickup truck and traveled to the local Trading and Exchange Post. He walked directly to the counter, purchased two boxes of #5 twenty gauge shot, and one box of rifle shells. He entered his truck and departed from the small city in Southeastern Ohio where he had lived for over four decades.

But we're not there yet. The previous day began with just the same mixture of routine and repetition. There was the groggy shower in the morning, the pre-departure rush, and the trip to the café for breakfast. And then I heard it on the radio behind the cash register. And maybe you were in California and you woke up to it or maybe you were woken up by it. In Berlin it caught you late in the afternoon right at the point you usually start looking forward to going home early from work. It interrupted your dinner in New Delhi. It stopped you on your way to bed in Sydney.

And I was caught in a moment, and time seemed to stop, but it really didn't. Time continued; it had just become inadequate for measuring this experience. I was still standing by that radio, listening with a mixture of determination and abandonment already having deliberately forfeited belief in what I was hearing. I arrived at a television just in time to not believe that I was watching the first tower fall and only later learning but still not believing, my mind refusing to believe, even if my memory will later remember, this is the second tower that is falling.

It was a Tuesday.

Even though I was hundreds of miles away from the attack sites, everyone wanted to know I was okay. Friends from around the globe contacted me. Many of them had never been to the US and, to them, Philadelphia was agonizingly close to both New York City and Washington, D.C. Even for those who were aware of the distance, it didn't matter. I've never been held more constantly in the thoughts of my friends and family. They all wanted to know I was okay.

Within a few hours, everyone knew I was okay. I thanked everyone and chuckled at their poor sense of geography which had

65

precipitated many of the calls. I scoffed at the fears of friends and relatives, and only later did I understand that this slight show of disdain was much easier than admitting my own ignorance and my own fear. Despite the continual influx of "'new information" on the attacks I was unsure about the security of my friends and loved ones. When I spoke to my grandmother that afternoon, she was decided: I never should have left home. I should have remained in the small Midwestern city in which I had been raised.

Being brown in the Midwest can be difficult. As one of few Latin-American families in my small corner of Ohio I had dealt with racial stereotypes for longer than I could remember. Indeed in the large hamlet removed fifty miles from Kentucky and thirty miles from West Virginia, racism hung in the air like a pungent odor. An early memory: I'm at the low-rent apartment complex where my family lives. On the standard Department of Housing and Urban Development playground I try to make myself understood in English. I've acquired the language quickly. The words come well ordered, but the accent will take years to quit my tongue. This is one of my few memories of linguistic frustration and inability. The other children are new and as interested in me as I am in them. The most inquisitive child of the group asks why I "speak funny." "Because I am from Nicaragua," I say.

The same child asks: "From where?"

Another interrupts: "Niggeragua?"

A third, with astonishment: "So you're a nigger?"[1]

I don't even know to say no.

I'm a nigger before I even know what it means, before I even know the disgust that accompanies the term. I later learn in that silent and all-accepting manner of children that this "word'" is less a signifier of my racial identity and more a mark of racial opprobrium. When I hear this word, which in the mouths of children from whom I first heard it had yet to ripen in its hatefulness, I'm not even furious.

When I later challenge this terminal classification, the kids in my neighborhood don't even bother to switch the racial epithet they hurl

---

1 In this essay, my use of charged racial language is meant to reflect accurately my experiences and the cultural currency of these terms and not as a means of glorifying racism or the terms it employs.

at me. At this time there's no better category of racial categorization.
— There are not enough Latinos to establish the critical mass necessary for either the introduction or the sustenance of "Spic," or "Wetback," or "Bean" or even "Goddammed Mexican" — this will come later but I will be an adult and only an itinerant visitor to the Midwest by then.

When informed of their mistake, my peers don't understand the difference and they don't care enough to listen to the labored explanations of racial identity with which I'm still unfamiliar. My strange-sounding name and dark eyes and hair are all the confirmation they need. My white mother and my too-light skin, cause and seal of the racially mixed union from which I came, only increase their disdain. They are young enough to believe it unnecessary to understand the fine lines of racial hate yet ignorant enough to unwaveringly believe in racism's existence.

This is where I grow up. There are no burning crosses. No threats are made to my family. The other children continue to talk to me. Times have changed. The elementary school down the road still has "colored only" bathrooms in its basement, but they've been desegregated for years and probably decades; another child informs me that I may pee where I wish. These same children, my peers, likewise teach me everything else that a young boy in America's Heartland needs to know. I learn to dislike Chinks and Gooks and I learn that if it's not them, it's the faggots. I learn to shift from one collection of racial slurs, one set of stereotypical expectations, and one trope-bound way of seeing the world to another with the same ease of a bilingual child seamlessly shifting mother tongues. I learn to fit in by hating the same people.

As I grow older, we talk about these things less, but their apparent absence only makes the racism more insidious. Our lack of discussion is testament, not to the correction of prejudice, but rather to our attainment of proficiency whose proof is so assured that its substance finds and needs find only irregular display. When my bus driver asks how "I got all the sun," I do not answer. When my last name is stripped of its mellifluence by mouths that refuse to pronounce the foreign sounds, I respond meekly. When my first name is mutilated and spit back at me as "Oreo" or even "Radiator," I remain silent. These are the memories I recall when my grandmother tells me late in the afternoon of September 11th that I should be in the Midwest. Indeed, these memories immediately collect and condense into a simple thought. The thought arrives so suddenly and clearly that I might have even spoken it aloud. And while my grandmother is speaking about terrorist attacks, I'm thinking: "Please don't let it be brown people."

When I came to the East Coast I thought I had shed much of my previous identity. At an elite private liberal arts college located in the affluent suburbs of Philadelphia, I started learning how to culturally pass. At the prestigious institution of higher education that prided itself on its ethnic diversity, my Latin heritage no longer qualified me as exotic. Coming from a rural area in the Midwest, however, was practically incredible.

With little option, I embraced my ignorance of diversity and quickly sought to amend the disagreeable belief systems that I had brought with me. Through a self-designed and rapid program of cultural immersion, I set out to replace my caricatured stereotypes. I sought those experiences whose absence had enabled both my ignorance and the prejudices I had learned. My Jewish roommate fascinated me. I'd never known a Jew before, but I never told him this. While plenty of my new peers were exploring the wiles of sex, drugs, and alcohol I was engaged in a different sort of social experiment designed to let me understand myself by learning to understand others. I was in large part motivated by the fear of rejection. I understood that my thoughts and beliefs were capable of forestalling my entry into the society in which I now lived. I knew it was important for me to question and examine the foundations upon which these beliefs stood. My abandonment of the Midwest taught me nothing so much as how thoroughly I had become a bigot.

I had initially assumed that the replacement of these prejudices would not be that difficult. I believed I could learn about Asian cultures in the same way that I had learned to eat a baked artichoke or read French literature. Having learned the motions of hate in order to fit in, I spent college learning the humanist creed of acceptance through the same observational skills that had enabled my adaptation to the Midwest.

When my grandmother wishes I were back in the Midwest, a land whose consistencies I believed to have already escaped by September 11th, 2001, I am still hoping that brown people are not responsible for the attacks. Not for myself, but rather for all the brown people in the U.S. who are "ethnic" or "minorities," and ever increasingly hyphenated into that taxonomical chimera of the "ethnic minority." As much as I'm afraid of further terrorist attacks, I'm more afraid of the consequences if the attacks were made by brown people. I know that the worst that I can expect is silent distrust and hidden frustration. Still insulated by the nearly ideal society of my college, I do not really expect to experience any reproach. I am afraid for those living in areas in which the hate is more malignant and excitable than even the small city in which I was raised.

Although I acquired my prejudices in the Midwest, it would be foolish to assume the insistent misunderstanding of prejudice might be localized to any area. In all my travels, I've confronted bigotry without ever having sought it. I've listened to people in Texas who promised me they could smell African blood and made the acquaintance of doctors in Minnesota who insisted on the biological inferiority of certain races. I've spent time in Massachusetts at almost completely Caucasian boarding schools in almost completely Caucasian towns where the people thought equality of opportunity was a goal our nation has reached. These beliefs were held in spite of the heavily impoverished Latin- and African-American communities that were less than five miles down the road. I've been denied admittance to Venezuelan discos because my friends were too dark complexioned and I've heard elderly Austrian woman hiss "Turk" and "Gypsy" as I pass. And, even in diverse Berkeley, California, I've experienced the prejudices based, as always, on "differences." I'd encountered this before 9/11 and I've also noticed it since.

But this essay would be worth little if its only goal were to recount the permutations of hate and misunderstanding I've experienced. Rather, my bias has exposed the naiveté of a belief that I once held deeply, that I could simply leave behind all the hate I had learned.

Before the sun had set on September 13th, 2001, Ralph Leroy Hutchinson had killed three squirrels, one less than the state limit, but exactly the amount needed to produce dinner for himself and his wife, my grandmother. Respectful in his own way of the tragedy that had occurred, he had spent a day and a half dealing with his shock. Then he had decided to view the terrorist attack as an invocation to in his own words, "live while the living was good" and to "not let no damned Arabs ruin his retirement."

Although I am ashamed of the crass manner in which he expressed his views and yet, in some small degree, admire my grandfather's ability to endure and overcome the tragedies, I know that endurance is easier when it does not require change. Complex situations are seldom resolved through simple solutions. There is no single lesson to be learned from Sept. 11. I do not doubt that this wound, still fresh, will continue to teach us much more as it continues slowly to heal.

By abandoning the Midwest I wanted to separate myself from the hate I had learned and to remedy as much of my ignorance as possible; I thought I could exculpate myself. In this era of the self-analytical individual, I failed to realize that I needed, not only to make a difference, in myself, but also in the world. September 11th didn't make me feel like an American, it made me feel like a person, not a citizen of the United States, but a member of humanity. Yet for all this consequent solidarity that many of us felt, Sept. 11 helped me to acknowledge the multiplicity of racial, religious, national, cultural heritages that define us, heritages often masqueraded and reduced through the negative rhetoric of difference. I became aware of many of the challenges in the world today, challenges we must face not in spite of but precisely because of their difficulty.

Over the last two years I have had the opportunity to partake of experiment, an experiment that is in many ways a more refined version of the one I undertook in college. With approximately 600 residents from 80 countries, International House Berkeley is a unique living environment that takes the world as its model. During my time here, I've come across much misunderstanding of myself and the multiple cultural heritages I embrace. I have come to realize that we are often limited not so much by our ignorance as by our supposed knowledge. This difficult and ongoing process of seeing myself from dissimilar viewpoints has provided me with a valuable perspective on both my achievements and my limitations as a member of the world.

Life is not perfect at International House; we all come here with our prejudices and biases. To leave them behind would be impossible. Still, the challenges we encounter and collectively surmount at International House serve as a testament to both the necessity of cultural exchange and the progress that is possible in the world. Joe Lurie, the Executive Director of International House, Berkeley, often reminds us that if the world were perfect, there would be no need for International House. And while events such as Sept. 11 can alter the world by presenting the extreme consequences to which hate can lead, the daily challenge of confronting what we think we know is our only hope for improving ourselves, and our world. This is the mission of International House. It is at once an experiment and a vision of hope, now in its seventy-fifth year, that has only grown stronger since its inception.

A Vision of Hope

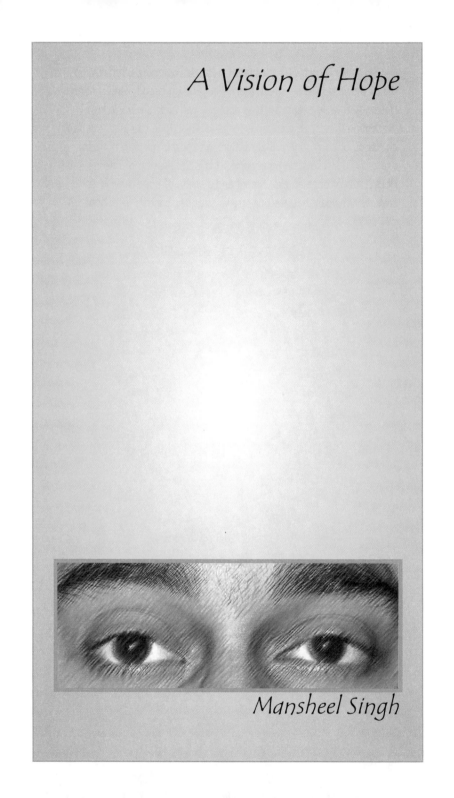

Mansheel Singh

I was born in Madera, a rural farming town in the San Joaquin Valley known as the heart of California. My father came to the United States from Panjab in the early seventies and settled in Madera in 1980. When he arrived in the U.S. people called him "Ayatollah" and "Ali Baba" because of his turban and beard, which are religious articles of the Sikh faith. These verbal attacks never got to him. He is solid to the core in his faith.

When I was growing up, "Pita Ji," as I call my father, told me about the great Sikh martyrs who were cut piece by piece by the invading Mughal tyrants, but who never gave up their Sikh faith. The history of the Sikh people is one of brutal persecutions and unparalleled courage.

Growing up in Madera I never did take the Sikh identity for all that it is. I kept long, uncut hair, which is a religious article of faith, and tied it into a joora or bun on top of my head and then covered it with a patka, or cloth covering. My appearance was definitely distinctive but I lived a normal life and attended a public school. I was the only Sikh boy in my school, and the kids always teased me. They used to grab my joora and try to pull it off. They called me all kinds of names: genie, rag head, camel back, Aladdin, Saddam, and sand nigger. You name it. I heard it. My classmates would tell me to "go back to your country – go back to Arabia" whenever they felt the need to insult me in an argument. In the restrooms, the other boys asked me if I was a boy or a girl. They figured that if I had long hair, I must have been a girl.

Despite these obstacles, I had the support of Pita Ji to keep me going. I felt like a normal kid who belonged in America. I remember having to recite the Pledge of Allegiance every morning in the class-room, including the words, "One nation, under God, indivisible, with liberty and justice for all." These words would later take on a different meaning for me.

On September 11, 2001, I walked into class wearing my patka over my joora just like any other day. But this was not like any other day. Everyone was gathered around the television watching the footage of the planes crashing into the twin towers. We could see smoke every-where and people jumping out of buildings. Then both towers collapsed and the New York skyline was covered in ash. The teachers started yelling across the halls, "We're under attack! We're under attack!"

Little did I know that their words would stick to me like a shadow. Within days, the television screens and newspaper headlines all tied the horrendous events to Osama bin Laden. Several days later, Balbir Singh Sodhi, a Sikh gas station owner, was shot and killed in Mesa, Arizona, in what was termed the first fatal hate crime triggered by September 11th. The man who killed him said that he was doing his patriotic duty. One Sikh man was arrested while sitting on the train during his commute from work. He was arrested because the other passengers suspected him of being a terrorist. The next day, his photo was on the front cover of local newspapers, next to Osama bin Laden. Across the country, hate crimes against Sikhs were on the rise. People associated the Sikh turban and beard with the terrorist image projected in the media. The nineteen men who hijacked the planes were all from Saudi Arabia and none of them wore turbans or had beards. I had no idea who Osama bin Laden was prior to the attacks but now, this is a name that has left deep scars on me. It is a name that I will never forget.

Over the past few decades, the Sikh community has grown in substantial numbers in the San Joaquin Valley even though I remained the only Sikh student in my school. Madera doesn't have a Gurdwara, or Sikh Temple. I did not receive support from the community in order to deal with the rise in hate crimes. Sikhs across the country were quick to do everything in their power to show their solidarity with America. Sikh-owned taxi cabs and gas stations were decorated with U.S. flags. Some Sikhs went so far as to wear red white and blue turbans. The Sikh community was making every effort to prove itself worthy of America. Everywhere I turned, Sikhs were telling people that we are not Muslims; we had nothing to do with the attacks and we are proud to be American. Although I felt it was important to tell people that Sikhs are not Muslims, I also felt it was important not to allow the blame to be directed at Muslims either.

A week after the Sept 11th attack, I was waiting to get picked up after school when a student driving by yelled, "Hey terrorist! Go home." There were many people watching and I wasn't sure how to react. I did what my Pita Ji told me to do whenever people say mean things: ignore them and keep going. As the only Sikh in my school, I felt a duty to represent myself appropriately. I wanted to lash out in anger but I could not find the words instead, I just let the hurt and anger sit inside.

It wasn't easy. How could I possibly tell every single person there that the Sikhs had nothing to do with the terrorist attacks? Most people have never heard of Panjab, let alone Sikhi. The comfort I felt before living in America was gone.

Most young kids in Panjab wear the patka only as young children. It is expected that all Sikh boys and girls wear a turban by the time they reach the teenage years. In the U.S., it is hard for young Sikhs to maintain the full Sikh identity. Many Sikh boys and girls cut their hair because they can not bear the abuse from fellow classmates. Many Sikh parents allow and even promote this "integration" because they want their kids to be successful in America. Some Sikh parents fear that long hair, beards and turbans are an obstacle in America, preventing their children from reaching their full potential. My Pita Ji taught me otherwise. He taught me that standing up for one's beliefs is an obligation that we must all face.

It wasn't easy for me anywhere after the attacks. In the classroom, students threw paper wads at my patka. In the halls, they threw pencils and more paper wads at me. Being a sophomore in high school meant that my beard had started to grow substantially. As I walked to class, students yelled, "bin Laden." As soon as I turned around, everyone acted as if nothing had happened. Once again, I had to hold my anger inside.

Every day I came home and looked at the photo of the great Sikh martyr, Bhai Taru Singh Ji. Bhai Taru Singh Ji was offered all the wealth he desired by the Mughal tyrants in exchange for converting to Islam and cutting his hair. He refused and was punished by having his scalp ripped off his head. He endured this torture but he never gave up his Sikh faith.

In November 2001 the school organized a school wide forum and asked me to speak on a panel about the September 11th attacks. I spoke to an audience of two hundred and told them about the Sikh religion. It didn't help. Kids continued to yell "bin Laden" at me at the top of their lungs across the campus. I could no longer eat lunch outside. I received numerous threats from other students but I kept Pita Ji's advice in mind and tried to ignore them.

I finally reached a point where I could no longer continue. I decided that I had to embrace the full Sikh identity. I decided to wear the full Sikh turban to school.

I remember the first day that I walked into school wearing the Sikh turban. I received the first reaction from a group of "Suerenos," a south side gang. They shouted, "Osama... raghead!" That wasn't exactly what I was hoping for, but I knew that I had to keep on going. Both the students and teachers treated me like I was a stranger. Most of my "friends" stopped talking to me. The only solution old friends would offer was to "cut your hair." People in the community told me to stop wearing the turban and to just do my best to fit in. My dastar or turban, was to them a symbol of terror. This, along with my long flowing dhari or beard, were ultimate acts of disloyalty.

I was walking home from school one day when a group of first graders started shouting "Osama" and impersonating the character Apoo from the Simpsons. What are you supposed to tell little first graders when you can't get people your own age to understand you? It was evident to me that the post September 11th hysteria generated by the media would leave lasting impressions on the coming generations. I vowed that I would never give up my identity just because people called me names. I started shutting myself off from people.

Once while driving on the way to a field trip, one of the teachers asked me if Sikhs also believe in a jihad or holy war. The history of the Sikhs reveals a people who fought against injustice and only engage in war when all means of redressing a wrong has failed. Sikhs are never oppressors. Someone who calls himself a Sikh and who acts in a tyrannical manner is not a true Sikh. And yet everywhere I turned, in my school, at the grocery store, at the local Wal-Mart, people were associating me with the oppressive Taliban. I didn't know who to have anger against, the Taliban or the Maderans next door. I felt betrayed.

On November 1, 2002, as I was walking on campus with one of my teachers, another teacher approached us. He had a big grin on his face. He suddenly grabbed my beard, tugged it hard and chuckled, "Hey, are you a member of the Taliban?" I was so angry I couldn't move. I looked him in the eye wondering what to say. He was an elderly man and I really didn't expect him to make such an inappropriate comment.

I did what Pita Ji told me to do: ignore his comments. I wanted to knock that man down off his feet right then and there but my obligations to the Sikh identity pulled me in the other direction. The principal and the school board immediately wrote letters assuring me that this was an isolated incident and not reflective of the school. It really got me thinking; some ignorant students associated me with the terrorists and here this ignorant teacher was doing the same. What was I supposed to do?'

I have come to realize what Bhai Taru Singh Ji represented and why he did what he did. I have come to realize the source of Pita Ji's strength.

The events of September 11, 2001, and the way Americans and the people of Madera reacted towards me opened my eyes and brought about a new consciousness within me. Out of all of this, I have found rewards beyond measure, beyond words. Everything that Pita Ji used to tell me about making sacrifices for one's beliefs all came together. I've learned who my real friends are and I've learned to recognize those who choose to alienate me and condemn my identity. I found my identity as a Sikh, something that I didn't know I had in me. I have found my home in Madera, in my heart.

A Need to Talk and Dream

Sarah Williams

"Ah, but a man's reach must exceed his grasp, or what's a heaven for?" wrote the poet Robert Browning in "Andea Del Sarto." He was able to capture the notion that only a vision of a better world is able to inspire humankind to exceed its ordinary capabilities and inclinations. Only if we fix our eyes on an objective which seems to us worthy of great effort can we sustain that effort through times when we feel unsure of the outcome, our motives, and our willingness to shoulder the burden of the compromises necessary to achieve the goal. We need both desire and focus and, as Robert Browning was suggesting, this holds true both in the physical and in the metaphysical realm. Anyone who has learned to ride a bike knows that if you look at the obstacle in the middle of the road, that is where the bike will take you. The proper technique is to keep the dangers in your peripheral vision but always to fix your gaze on where you want to be. The world is full of challenges, and we need to be able to navigate around them. Maybe we will need to adjust our balance, maybe change speed and direction from time to time; however, our primary focus should always be that particular point at which we want to arrive. Thus it is in the metaphysical realm also. To a large extent, life is a self-fulfilling prophecy. For those who see only barriers, problems, and conflicts, potholes always seem to be the *plat du jour*. For those of a positive mindset, problems are simply the inevitable corollary of setting oneself a worthwhile objective.

Setting your sights on a vision is not just a recipe for the goal-oriented achievers in this world, though. It's much more than that. It's an essential component of the struggle for a better, fairer, more peaceful world; a paradigm for addressing the social, political and cultural conflicts that seem to be bursting forth from our television screens and newspapers day in and day out. One of the main causes of conflict is not that people have conflicting interests, although sometimes this is the case, or that they have conflicting cultures, which is rarely the case. The main problem is that as a result of prejudice and stereotyping, people perceive that they have conflicting interests and cultures, and that perception, fueled by the grubby business of political coalition-building, can easily erupt into a full-blown conflict. Once this happens, the aptly-named "theater of conflict" opens to packed houses. Reaction begets counter-reaction, and in short order even those without pre-existing prejudices feel forced to identify themselves as being on one side of the line or the other.

An unfortunate but crucial example of this is the widening divide between the Islamic and Judeo-Christian worlds. Since the end of the 1970s, in countries such as Iran, Turkey, Palestine, Lebanon and Saudi Arabia, politicized forms of Islam have arisen in response to longstanding social and political problems. A long-term analysis of this trend shows that "Political Islam" is the most recent in a string of movements which have tried to address structural inequality and democratic deficit in the Middle East. Socialism had failed, Arab Nationalism had failed, and alternative political philosophies offered by the West were either not feasible or had no credibility. The international community, in particular the West, was seen, with varying degrees of justification, to have contributed to rather than ameliorated the problems, and so the Islamic world turned inward, finding within Islam precepts to which it could culturally relate. Political operators like Ayatollah Khomeini found that Islamic texts could be bent for instrumental purposes in the pursuit of power. As a result, the perception has arisen, from those outside such movements, that somehow the protest is an expression of Islam. The reality, however, is that the reverse is true. The conflict is not an expression of Islam; Islam is a mode of expression of the conflict. If circumstances had been different, Christianity could have been reinterpreted as an equally useful political credo. Indeed, during the Crusades, it was so. Judaism, of course, has been politically utilized to underpin notions of statehood in Israel. However, ideas like those of Harvard political scientist, Samuel Huntington. In his "Clash of Civilizations" with its talk of fundamental antagonisms between the religious traditions, have started to gain currency, and there are feelings in the West that Islam is a danger per se. This corresponds to a widespread belief in the Islamic world that the West intends domination and is therefore a threat to the East. For terrorist leaders like Osama Bin Laden, this has offered a golden opportunity to simultaneously acquire power and wage war against his enemies, which are not limited to the West but include Shia Islam and the Saudi dynasty. The high water mark of his campaign on the 11th of September 2001 provoked a US-led response which has further inflamed the sense in the Muslim world that the West is on a "crusade" against Islam, and although the successful campaign to oust Al Qa'ida from Afghanistan seems to have had some success in achieving its objective, we are now dealing with a multi-headed hydra. The fractured Al Qa'ida has splintered and grafted itself onto other Islamic nationalist groups which have re-acted to this influence by broadening their objectives. No longer confined to state borders, groups such as Jemaah Islamiya and Laskar Jihad in Indonesia and Lashkar-e-Taiba in Kashmir are increasingly buying into the Al Qa'ida vision of a broad territorial reach for Islamic government.

In domestic terms, both within and without the West, this has translated into an increase in prejudice and stereotyping of the "other" and, to use my motorbike metaphor, there are worrying signs that we are heading, both on a global and a personal level, towards a huge pothole of antagonism, distrust and conflict. The European Monitoring Centre on Racism and Xenophobia has blamed the British media for using negative stereotypes of Muslims and portraying asylum seekers as "the enemy within" after September 11. The same criticism might be leveled at the USA. The Council on American-Islamic Relations recently lambasted Fox TV for their depiction of Arab-Americans on the show "24." In this season's storyline, Muslim terrorists kidnap the Secretary of Defense and plot a "nuclear holocaust." In Canada, similar problems exist; for example, October of last year, a Muslim man, Kassim Mohammed, was arrested for videotaping Toronto's landmark CN Tower. There simply as a tourist, Kassim aroused suspicion for the plain fact of being a Muslim looking at a notable skyscraper.

As a middle-class British woman, when it comes to prejudice and stereotyping, I've usually found myself on the greener side of the fence. My feelings about conflict tend to come from other people's reports or abstract theorizing... I'm probably the conflict resolution equivalent of a "champagne socialist," which in the British vernacular means someone who worries about inequality from the comfortable vantage point of privilege.

Last summer, though, I had the tiniest taste of what it might feel like to be walking on the no-so-sunny side of the street. As an adjunct to my academic program, I visited Israel and Palestine. I was interning with The Rebuilding Alliance, a non-profit whose objective is the rebuilding of demolished Palestinian homes and schools. I was there to research how we could rebuild two homes in East Jerusalem which had been demolished for planning regulation infractions. The families had been living in a tent beside the rubble. The rebuilding work was going to be done by multi-faith (including secular) teams of Israelis, Palestinians and other internationals, and part of the objective of the exercise was reconciliation and healing. Although our work was controversial in some quarters, there was no suggestion that the people who we were trying to help were or had been involved in violence or with organizations engaged in violent struggle. However, from the moment that I arrived at Ben Gurion Airport, I felt as if I was perceived as some kind of threat to Israel. It was a strange experience for me. Although I didn't go into an explanation of my internship work with the woman at the immigration desk, I made the mistake of saying I was a Rotary Peace Scholar. No, I wasn't Jewish. Worse still, I had just flown in from Cyprus where I had attended a month-long peace symposium. Immediately, the woman's attitude changed. The questions became more curt, and before long she left to find someone to take me off for an in-depth interview. I started to remember the stories I had been told about the British peace activist who had been held in detention by airport security for three weeks now. Thankfully, I had flown in from Cyprus with three Jewish friends from the symposium who, as soon as they saw me being led to a side room, intervened and vouched for me. Their support seemed to verify that I was not a likely enemy of the state and I was allowed through.

It was a strange experience for me. I've never felt remotely like anyone's enemy, so the idea of being viewed with suspicion was uncomfortable. In terms of prejudice or stereotyping, though, this was a very minor experience. Compared to experiences of people all over the world, day in and day out, at the hands of those who see them as different or threatening because of the color of their skin, their dress, their religion or some other characteristic, this was nothing. There are those who say that what I experienced was simply the sensible caution of a country which has sustained great losses as a result of terrorism, and it is not difficult to put myself in the shoes of an Israeli citizen. I too would want those protecting my borders to be vigilant. Having said that, I don't think that the officers I encountered thought that I represented any kind of physical threat to anyone. It was more a form of defensiveness in response to a perceived implicit criticism. The lesson for me, though, was to do with the way that I felt, not the rightness or wrongness of how the immigration officials had reacted. I had been treated as part of "the other" for the first time in my comfortable privileged life and it felt like a slap in the face. The feeling stayed with me for the duration of my stay in that beautiful, troubled country. I perceived suspicion of me everywhere, whether it was there or not. By the end of my seven-week trip, I had started to relax a little and became increasingly able to understand that my own reaction was creating an unhelpful dynamic. It was an important insight for me into the way in which people can be brought into a conflict against their will, without initial animosity towards the other and then find their feelings are so engaged that they become part of the problem, not the solution.

But is it inevitable that misunderstanding and prejudice leads to a more dangerous conflict? Is it inevitable that the Muslim and non-Muslim worlds are set on a collision course? Absolutely not. However, we have to ensure that this cleavage between peoples does not become a self-fulfilling prophecy. From the experience I have described, I learned that it was through connection with those people that I had come to think of as "the others" that my feelings started to subside and be replaced with an appreciation of the complexity and diversity of Israel and its people. Within the broader political context this is a moment in history where it is essential that we look not at the dangers that surround us, but at the future that we can jointly enjoy if we are able to diminish the fear and mistrust threatening to unseat us. We must start mentally to inhabit a world in which we share a larger human identity; one which can accommodate the other identities which are also important to us, one in which we can accept that problems are inevitable and that, through their solution, we can find the key to progress. We have to engage with each other, and we have to dream together.

Looking first at the engagement aspect of my proposal: "social communication" theorists such as Habermas suggest that our social identity does not emerge from the convergence of pre-existing interests but through socialization and argumentative consensus building. Since as we have seen, the crystallization of identity carries significant consequences, reality is to a large extent created by norms, ideas and perceptions. Consider Rwanda. If we know that during the genocide in 1994, a view of reality was being constructed by the Hutu leadership for the ordinary Hutu population whereby the small improvements in their life that had been made since democratization were about to be taken away from them by a Tutsi conspiracy. If we understand that such construction occurred within a historical continuum in which Hutus had been systematically discriminated against in favor of the Tutsi population as part of a Belgian colonial policy of "divide and rule," then we can start to question interpretations of events which point to ancient tribal enmity or behavioralism. We start to understand that the actions of the Hutus took place within a matrix which had been historically and strategically created for them. From the point of view of conflict resolution rather than conflict creation, we can also start to see that where parties in conflict can increase their perception of the structures of understanding within which they and their adversaries are operating, they may be capable of seeing the conflict within a larger context. This enlarged perception may help them to imagine a future in which the survival of one group is not inimical to the survival of another. Even when we cannot emotionally accept another viewpoint, temporarily inhabiting the perspective of our adversary helps us to recognize certain shared human characteristics.

Following this logic, reality cannot be changed unless perceptions are changed. However, if perceptions are malleable, then there is potential for the landscape to look very different. Sometimes the change has its roots in unilateral action. For example, the Cold War, which pitted the ideology of capitalism against communism, created an international political structure which constrained the decisions of political actors across the globe. It affected the policy of every nation in virtually every aspect. Each side perceived the other as presenting a mortal threat, and this was part of reality for almost half a century. In what seems now like the twinkling of an eye, the edifice of communism vanished. The former communists were still present, the guns and tanks still existed, but reality had changed in a quantum leap. With his policies of Glasnost and Perestroika, Gorbachev changed the political reality of the entire world. Suddenly, to the West, the USSR did not pose the same level of threat and this opened the way to interactions that had previously seemed impossible.

At other times, the action which prompts the change is symbolic. When President Sadat of Egypt stepped into the Israeli Knesset in 1977, after decades of inter-state conflict, he changed the reality of the Middle East. Previously, Israelis had been unable to consider Egypt as a potential partner for peace. With Sadats gesture of entering the "enemy heartland," a re-evaluation took place which led to a marked change in the political landscape.

More often though, perceptions change through the act of communication itself. Harold Saunders, Director of International Affairs at the Kettering Foundation, believes that through a dialectical experience, carried out in public, conflicts of identity can be transformed into conflicts of interest. The former tend to consist of institutionalized relationships of enmity, whereas the latter are much more amenable to resolution through negotiation. Without communicative engagement, attempts to resolve differences between various groups often break down under the weight of the traditional jousting between symbolic issues. Despite the obvious risks, Saunders advocates that public deliberation over time can be the most viable means by which social relationships of enmity can be transformed. Often within a conflict, the dominant narrative encapsulating the rationale for the struggle is established by more powerful actors, usually those with large interests at stake. Repeated often enough by sources having weight and authority within a social group, these utterances become articles of faith which define the contours of the conflict from the perspective of that group. There are many examples:

"Islam is a violent religion,"

"Western culture is depraved and materialistic,"

"Immigrants are taking our jobs and endangering our culture,"

"Jews are mean and power-seeking,"

"Kosovan Albanians are uncivilized people who breed large numbers of children,"

"Serbs are an aggressive race."

Whatever the stereotype and no matter how disconnected it may be from the facts on the ground, it retains its rhetoric force and shapes the trajectory of the outcome.

While discourse contributes to and crystallizes a conflict, it also provides an important tool for resolving it and creating a sustainable society. The dominant narrative can be challenged by a free flow of accurate and constructive information. This allows for the counteracting of misperceptions, the identification of genuine interests through the access to expression of otherwise-unheard voices and the creation of consensus through debate in place of ideological or interest-driven domination. A rich and diverse dialectic contributes to the dissolution of stereotypes, both within one's own group and amongst the other groups represented within the discussion, and it provides a constructive environment for the conflict resolution, since it increases the level of actual listening that takes place. Furthermore, it generates creative thinking. As George Bernard Shaw succinctly put it, "if you have an apple and I have an apple and we exchange apples, then each of us will still have one apple... but if you and I exchange ideas, then each of us will have two ideas"!

The second aspect of my proposal is the necessity of vision. "I have a dream," said Martin Luther King, and so powerful was his expression of that dream that, generations after the Civil Rights Movement secured (roughly) equal political rights for blacks in the US, his vision still inspires those who seek to connect, not with a person of or without color, but with another human being. Another great visionary, Nelson Mandela, negotiated the dismantling of the apartheid regime in South Africa. With his belief that "the common ground is greater and more enduring than the differences that divide," he settled an agreement on universal suffrage and became not just South Africa's first black president but the first president of South Africa committed to the well-being of all South Africans. What made him stand out from other South African leaders was precisely his vision of a state that belongs equally to all its different peoples, nations, and tribes, whether Afrikaans, English, or Zulu. Being himself a leader belonging to the Xhosa-speaking people, he eventually transcended the idea of ethnic nationalism, and he attracted Indians, Jews, and other segments of the multi-cultural population to the cause. Whatever the problems that South Africa has since encountered, few people would argue with the proposition that the power of Mandela's vision and commitment helped to steer that country away from imminent tragedy and towards a brighter future.

What this engagement and vision also requires is good leadership… national leaders, community leaders, spiritual leaders and role models who look to the next generation and not to the next election. Unfortunately, from where I'm standing they appear a little thin on the ground at the moment. In view of the immediacy of the situation, I would suggest that we cannot wait for them to appear. Politics is far too important to be left to the politicians. As Ghandi said, "Be the change you want to see." None of us can change the world at a stroke. However, we can play our part in contributing to a reality that recognizes individuals rather than stereotypes. We can stand up to the cynics who tell us that the in the "real world" we must focus on our own security, regardless of its expense to others and we can proclaim the power of people and ideas in contrast to the power of guns and money. There is an urgent need to focus on that which unites humanity rather than that which divides it. It is now up to us all to rise to the challenge.

Pictured left to right: Tammy A. Scott, Betsey Warrick (Judges), Sam Keninger, Mansheel Singh, Janet Dollacker, Aurelio Perez, Peter J. Robertson (Vice Chairman, Chevron), Liliane Koziol (Vision of Hope Project Director, I-House Director of Programs) and Mark Massoud; front: Karen Erlichman, Vandana Kapur and Karen LeFeber. A lithograph created for International House by David Goines, depicting a dove, representing peace, transcending a helmet of war, was presented to Peter Robertson.

ACKNOWLEDGMENTS. This project was successfully accomplished through the dedicated work of many people from close and afar who helped in all the steps of the project. For that we are very grateful. Particular thanks go to Linda Blum, Firoozeh Dumas, Charlene Raimondi, Tammy A. Scott, and Betsey Warrick who served as judges. The commitment of the I-House Program Office staff, especially my Assistant Larnie Macasieb and the 2004-2005 Rotary Peace Scholars Program Coordinators, was exemplary. Finally, we would like to single out Sheila Arado's professionalism in ensuring the integrity and confidentiality of the contest process.

STATISTICS. There was a total of 34 entries from 20 men and 14 women representing 11 countries (China, Germany, India, Iran, Japan, Netherlands, Pakistan, Spain, United Kingdom, Nigeria, and US). Ten participants were non-native English speakers. For those who were students, we had 17 majors represented, and the community members came from 14 different professions. Not all the participants resided in the Bay Area. Two I-House alumnae and two residents were among the winners of the contest.

Vision of Hope Essay Collection Evaluation

We would appreciate your responses to the following questions. Please add additional pages if necessary.

How meaningful and/or useful to you was this booklet of essays?

What aspects of the essays were of interest to you? (Please check as many as applicable.)

o   The narrative description and explanation of the bigotry and/or stereotyping experienced by the writer in the wake of the September 11 attacks.

o   The description of how the writer reacted to the experiences.

o   The tips from the writers on positive ways to counteract stereotyping and prejudice.

What other or additional topics or areas would you have liked to have seen listed or covered by the essays?

Do you plan to use this booklet as a resource in the course of your work?   o Yes   o No

What aspect will you use or how would you use it?

Suggestions and recommendations:

Name (optional):

Field of expertise or profession:

Thank you for returning your completed evaluation to:

Liliane Koziol, Director of Programs
International House
2299 Piedmont Avenue, Berkeley, CA 94720-2320
510-642-9460
email: lkoziol@berkeley.edu